Hey, Girlfriend!

Live Passionately Real

By Michelle Neujahr
Edited by Vickie Ross

Beaver's Pond Press, Inc.
Edina, Minnesota

Hey, Girlfriend! Live Passionately Real
©2001 by Michelle Neujahr.

All Rights Reserved. No part of this book may be reproduced, stored in a retrieval system, or transmitted in any form or by any means–electronic, electrostatic, magnetic tape, mechanical, photocopying, recording or otherwise–without permission in writing from the author.

Book Design and Typesetting by Mori Studio.

ISBN: 1-931646-01-5

Library of Congress Catalog Card Number: 2001090187

First Edition

Printed in the United States of America.

04 03 02 01   5 4 3 2 1

Address Orders to:

Beaver's Pond Press, Inc.

5125 Danen's Drive
Edina, Minnesota 55439-1465
www.beaverspondpress.com

To Jessica

my first and forever girlfriend

Special Thanks...

This book would not have been completed without the encouragement, commitment and endless support of my editor and dearest girlfriend, Vickie Ross, to whom I offer my deepest appreciation and affection.

Thanks, Girlfriend—you are awesome!

Acknowledgements

I would not have been able to write this book without the love and constant support of my family. They have loved me and believed in me each step of the way. My love goes to David, my husband and best friend, for always being my biggest fan. To Brandon, my first-born son, for "seeing" my book and believing in me even when I didn't. To Brittni, my daughter and littlest girlfriend, for your excitement and interest in my writing. And to Brady, my little guy, for all the mornings you sat on my lap as we wrote together at the computer. I am forever grateful for all of you—I love you with my whole heart!

Many people contributed their time, energy and experiences to this manuscript. I appreciate all of you. My love goes out to my mom, Diane Stores; my sister, Jessica Arellano; and all my girlfriends: Jean Peterson, Sonya Skinner, Patsy Keech, Mary Lower, Julie Ann Vingers, Janna Krammer, Maurya Laqua, Sheree Vincent, Susan Secord, Janel Anderson, Terese Mudrick, Sandy Tevlin and Pam Nelson.

And most importantly, I want to thank you, the reader. I appreciate you and acknowledge you. You are Awesome!

Chapters for Hey, Girlfriend!

Our Relationships
    The Girlfriend Thing 3
    Let's Be Friends. 9
    Let's Call a Truce to the Mommy War 17
    Be Genuine 23
    A Computer Can't Hug Ya! 29
    Lonely in a Room Full of People..................... 33
    Let's Have Coffee 39
    Competition—We Are Not Out to Win! 43

Our Families
    Be Silly... 51
    Time Out 55
    I Missed It 61

Be Spontaneous 67
I Didn't Just Want to Run Away From Home–I Did! 73
Go Away for the Holidays 79

Our Obsessions

Stop Obsessing 85
Business or Busyness 91
Won't Work for Chocolate Anymore! 97
I Work Like A Dog—Probably Harder Than a Dog. . . . 101
Get Out of the Box 107
Accept, Accept, Accept 115
The Joneses Aren't Happy Either! 123

Ourselves

The "No" Nightie 131
Let Go—Life Is Way Too Short! .139
Dream Out Loud! 145
Be Gentle to Yourself Each Day .153
Exercise—Ya Gotta! 159
Make Friends With Your Body—
    No Matter What Size It Is 165

Our Relationships

The Girlfriend Thing

The girlfriend thing started when I made a decision to start a home-based business. My hobby turned into a business and broadened my circle of friends. I had never had a lot of people in my life. Yet as I began to open my home and my heart to my business, "girlfriends" came into my life!

It was strange to be surrounded by people all of a sudden. I had spent most of my life being isolated. I'd never allowed myself many friends. I had a few close friends but wasn't much into the social thing. I professed not to care and yet I did care. I wanted people in my life. I just didn't know how to go about it.

I didn't start out trying to make more friends with my business. It just happened as the business grew. I was in a service-oriented business where people were constantly in my home. This was new to me. I had never had many people in my home—now there were people everywhere. It was a shock to my isolated system.

As my business began to grow, I grew and others wanted to do what I was doing. I fell into managing a team. I was unsure about this direction at first but felt it would be an awesome experience. It was. I now could grow my business and help others as well. I began training new consultants and building a unit. I enjoyed each one and continued encouraging others to join the team.

After I had been recruiting for a while, the first two "girlfriends" came. They were outgoing, wild women who were full of life! I loved them from the start. They immediately called me "girlfriend"—something no one had ever called me before. It felt strange but comfortable.

As we got to know each other, we began to function as a team and our standard greeting became "Hey, Girlfriend." When someone yelled out across the room "Hey, Girlfriend," my heart would do a little dance. They were calling me—I was the girlfriend!

The "girlfriend thing" was encouraging. It made me feel young all over again. I had never been part of a group growing up; I never fit in or had many friends. Yet there I was—27 years old and feeling like a kid. I had girlfriends. I was a part of something. I fit in and they loved me—it was fantastic! You see, when I call you friend (hence "girlfriend"), I feel positive toward you and, therefore, I'm not thinking of being competitive.

Being in sales can be competitive. People within the same unit often compete and hurt one another. We overcame that by creating a non-competitive environment. We enjoyed being part of "the girlfriend thing" and it grew. We encouraged one another, helped out at each other's events and we grew. We were the "Girlfriends" and we were awesome!

My girlfriends taught me to open up, live life and reach for the stars! In fact one of my girlfriends calls me continually just to encourage me to get on with this book.

The other thing that happened with the "girlfriend thing" was it spread. It spread to others and it spread to my other relationships. It was as if the simple words "Hey, Girlfriend" had opened up a door in my heart that had been closed. All of a sudden I started to think of women as girlfriends, not enemies. For way too long I thought women were the enemy. They were not to be trusted and definitely not to befriend. Yet as I said the words "Hey Girlfriend" over and over to my unit, something awesome happened. My heart began to change and I actually began to believe they were my GIRLFRIENDS!

I encourage you to be a "Girlfriend," too. Call your friends your "girlfriends" and watch yourself change. What we speak we become. We create an environment for openness and honesty, and we become closer, more confident and more connected.

We have new "girlfriends" today. As the word spread, we began to acquire more and more girlfriends. I'm meeting new girlfriends each and every day, and they challenge me to continue growing in my "girlfriend-hood."

I still fall into competition, put the walls up and run away. I still don't call my entire group of friends "girlfriend." And there are still some friends I'm afraid to get close to. My behavior makes me sad. I want to be more open and yet there are times I clam up. I don't like that part of me. I want to stay committed to being open and being willing to be a girlfriend!

Each and every day I'm becoming a girlfriend and I'm becoming me—uniquely and awesomely me. I am becoming exactly who God created me to be! As I become more me, I am more open to you.

I love ya, Girlfriend! And I encourage you to be a "girlfriend." As a girlfriend you will open up, be challenged and loved. We need one another. You go, Girlfriend! Read this book, become real with yourself, allow laughter in and be a "Girlfriend!"

Let's Be Friends

We need one another! We need women friendships! We have valuable insights and encouragement to give one another.

I appreciate the women in my life today because they help me. They challenge me to grow and they lift me up when I'm down. They help me sort out my life and they offer insight into my soul. I do the same for them. But it's taken many years for me to become comfortable with this process. It's an area I still struggle with.

Why are women friendships so hard? I don't know. For many years, I felt women were competition in my life. I found it easier to get along with men. I avoided women friendships and I isolated myself. I didn't want to get too close and I definitely didn't want to get hurt. So I stayed away.

I had many bad experiences in high school with girlfriends—I was hurt badly. So I built a wall and just hung out with the guys. I had a few friends but didn't get too close. I vowed I would never let a woman in again. I couldn't stand how women treated one another. I thought they were mean and cliquey and rude and competitive and I didn't want anything to do with them.

I have observed lots of pain in female relationships. I saw it in ninth grade and I see it today. We are guarded and afraid. We compete and we're phony. We don't want to let other people in. Yet we long for a girlfriend, a confidant, someone with whom we can share our soul and our daily struggles.

Many of you *do* have girlfriends. You are fortunate if you have friends in your life with whom you can be yourself and "do life" with. Thank them—they are a gift! Be grateful for the girlfriends in your life because they will help you become a better woman.

But if women relationships are hard for you, I encourage you to explore why. Are you afraid and insecure? Do you cover it up by saying, "I don't have time or I really don't want any female friendships"? Do you feel lonely and secretly wish you had more people in your life? Do you want to reach out to someone but are afraid of rejection? There are many reasons for keeping ourselves isolated and closed. We feel safe, protected from being hurt, and we don't have to be challenged by someone else's point of view.

How do you know being open to other women won't hurt you? You don't! There are no guarantees. You may get hurt. But you may really be blessed by having that person in your life. You won't know the opportunities that wait until you try.

There is a whole world of girlfriends out there waiting to be your friend. You have to decide. Do you want to be open to other women? Do you want to keep on going the way you are? Even if you already have a lot of friends, you can benefit from letting other women into your life.

For many years, I sought only people who thought just like I did. I couldn't handle anything or anyone that went against my way of thinking. I isolated myself and I hurt a lot of people in the process. I still feel sad over the relationships I destroyed back then, and I wish I could go back and repair them. I made huge mistakes and I live with regret. I know now that it is good to have people in my life who are different from me.

Differing opinions challenge us to look at life in a new way. We may not change our minds and think like our friends, but we open ourselves to new ideas. I have many friends whose beliefs are different from mine. These friends are valuable to me because they stretch me!

Sometimes these relationships stimulate great debate. We go back and forth and challenge each other. Yet because of the relationship and the love we have for one another, it's okay to disagree. I feel secure in who I am today. I'm starting to feel free enough to let the real me out regardless of who I'm with. I'm not perfect or totally there yet, but it's a beginning.

I want to be able to be who I am in all of my relationships and let others be who they are. That's how we grow.

We need other women! We need to have friends and we need to be a friend. We cannot grow in a closed environment. We need others to help us and to teach us. Sometimes they hurt us. But all these experiences help us grow. We are not meant to be isolated in this world. We are a part of a much bigger plan and we must be open to that plan.

Being open to other relationships can be very difficult. Relationships are hard, they require time, and they don't always work. They can be joy-filled—or they can be painful. Through it all you can grow.

And not every relationship we have is meant to last forever. Our lives change and we grow and we move. I believe sometimes people come into our lives for a season; we learn from that relationship and then it's over. It's okay; we don't have to have the same friends forever. Nor do we need 50 girlfriends; we don't have time for that many. Yet we all need a few safe people in our lives.

One of my goals for 1999 was to nurture two or three women friendships. I thought about this a great deal. Who would I choose? As I prayed about it I knew the ones I wanted to grow closer to. I'm glad to report that I am fulfilling my goal and I am growing. I have three unique and fairly new relationships in my life with people whom I love dearly. I have nurtured these friendships and it's really cool. I am learning that all female relationships are not full of competition and backbiting. We can actually be nice to each other and it works.

You may get hurt! It's painful when you do but you'll learn and you'll live through it. Just don't allow yourself the retreat of bitterness and isolation. I have done that all too often and it's lonely. I believe that when relationships are troubled or painful it's because we have something to learn. Maybe that difficult person was placed in our lives to teach us something. Take time to find out what that is. Be willing to look within and discover where you are being challenged. On the other hand, you may be in their life for *their* growth. You may be able to bring something to them that they need. We are often in each other's lives to sharpen and challenge each other.

That's how life works best. We touch other people's lives when they need it, and then we continue on. Some of those people will stay, some will go, and some will come in and out of our lives. Don't stay stuck in relationships that no longer enrich your life. It's okay to let go. You let go in love and then you create more space in your life for someone new. There should always be a flow of people in and out of your life.

We may be blessed with a lifelong friendship. Lifelong friends don't necessarily have to be in our life every day; but they're always in our hearts. We may not talk for a long time, but when we do it's as if we were never apart.

I have a friend like that from college. She and I only talk a few times a year, but when we talk—it's the highlight of my day! She's my cheerleader! She encourages me and loves me. I know she'd do anything for me as I would for her.

There are other relationships where we are so similar we feel we are on the same path. I have a friend like this, too. She and I have similar lives. We can relate to one another's thoughts and we are often going through the same thing at the same time. It never ceases to amaze me—I call her and she's going through the same thing I am. It's a little weird and yet it's a relationship that I value deeply. I feel, in some ways, she has become a sister to me.

Is being open to these types of relationships easy? NO! Will there be pain and struggles as we venture out and try to have better relationships with other women? YES! Will it be worth it? YES! It'll be worth it because you'll be free to explore new ways of thinking, you'll be open to those around you, and you'll become a participant in life, not an observer.

I know the benefits and I know I have a lot more to learn. I still crawl into my shell and hide, but I find that I stay there less than I used to. I'm learning to participate in life and the relationships around me.

Go, Girlfriend! You need friends and they need you. I need you. You are a valuable woman. You have much to offer and much to receive.

Go live and be a Girlfriend!

Let's Call a Truce to the Mommy War

After being an at-home mom for almost 10 years, I decided to go back to work. I was bored and frustrated with my life as it was. I felt sure I was missing something. It was time to venture into corporate America.

This decision came after almost a year of mulling it over, creating a resume and spending countless hours discussing it with everyone I knew. My husband and I decided that it was time and he supported me 100 percent.

I was scared to death. "What do I have to offer this big world?" I asked myself a million times. I had a college degree and some at-home business skills, but I had never worked in a corporate setting.

I spent months preparing a resume and getting the word out that I was looking for a job. I was off on a new journey. It was exciting. But finding a job was not the hard part. The hard part was the hurt that I experienced as a result of my friends' and family's reactions. I was shocked.

I never thought about the segmenting of women in our population before. I had just been home doing what I felt worked best for our family at the time. I had a circle of friends who were also home and we spent lots of time together. I didn't know that crossing the line to being a working mother would cause so much conflict.

I immediately began receiving way more input about my decision than I asked for. People were mortified that I would even consider going back to work when my youngest of three children was only 3. I received criticism and rejection from many of my so-called friends.

I was hurt deeply. I couldn't understand why I was feeling so confused. I know now that there are basically three groups of moms: the die-hard stay-at-homers, the part-timers and the full-time career moms. I do not mean to stereotype anyone; these groups simply serve as a guideline for my story.

My story did not have a happy ending. I continued to receive feedback from my at-home friends that was both cruel and uninvited. The part-timers seemed to think part time was a better option and my career friends supported me 100 percent. I actually developed relationships with new women during this time, women I had never connected with before.

As I struggled personally to overcome this rejection, I sat down and asked myself some tough questions: Would I treat a friend this way? Was I judgmental of the choices others made? Did I feel the way I had chosen to spend my days was the only answer?

I probed deep. As I looked at myself, I learned that there were definitely times when I had been judgmental and critical, feeling that somehow I was superior. Yet there had been many times when I felt completely inadequate and envied my working friends desperately.

I was embarrassed by my own behavior and thought it very fitting that now it had come back to bite me.

I got a job! After six interviews I accepted a position I thought would be the world. It was fun for a while, but this particular job was not for me.

I worked only three months, but during that time I learned a lot. I learned that women do what they do for many different reasons. What I saw over and over again was how we cut down other women if their choices are different from ours. Even though we all struggle with our own lives, it is easier to cut down someone else's choice rather than look at our own.

We need to call a truce to this Mommy War! It's destroying relationships and causing division among us. We need to be comfortable with the decisions we have made in our own life and be respectful of the decisions of those around us. We are no better for having a job or not having a job. We are all on different paths, at different times, and we are all doing the best we can with what we have at the moment.

Working women need to respect the at-home mom. We do work. We work very hard and we often don't receive any strokes for what we do. We're often insecure and uncomfortable around working women because we feel somehow less than or superior to. It's all such a lie. We each have a unique set of circumstances that make us who we are—our upbringing, our finances, our interests and who we were created to be. There are those who spent their whole life just dreaming of being a mom and it's all they have ever wanted. And there is nothing wrong with that.

At-home moms need to respect a working mother's right to work and support her in that decision. We need these women; society needs these women. And whether they want to work or have to work for financial reasons, they need to be supported.

It's never up to us to differentiate between those who want to work and those who have to. You need to know that whether you work outside the home or not, your children know your commitment and love for them.

I feel privileged to be at home again, but I'll never forget the lessons I learned through working full time. I will never again criticize any woman's decision about whether to work or not. I'll strive to keep my attitude in check. If I'm unhappy with what my life is at the moment, then it's up to me to change it. It's not up to me to analyze what others do with the lives they have been given or chosen.

Let's make a commitment to call a truce to the Mommy War. We do not need it and it won't help us. We are moms who love our children and who are doing the best we can each day to provide for them. We can love each other more wholly if we stop treating those who are different from us with such disrespect.

You'll open yourself up to many new relationships by not limiting yourself to people who are just like you. This was an awesome gift to me. I learned many new things from my working friends.

We have a lot to offer each other in our differences. Let's use it to make our journey as women more enjoyable for all of us.

Be Genuine

Let's be real! Let's stop pretending to be something we aren't. Let's not be a fake. Let's be real people with real lives.

We try too hard to make our lives perfect, to look good and to hide our warts. We all have warts, you know; yet we try our best not to reveal them. A friend of mine said to me the other day, "I would never want anyone to know my personal life. That's personal." I wanted to laugh out loud as I calmly nodded in agreement. All the while I was thinking, "I can't wait until she reads my book. She will die! She'll probably be embarrassed for me because stuff like this should never be shared." Who says we should keep quiet? Is it worth the work to pretend?

I don't believe it's worth it and I don't want to be something I'm not. I want to be real and genuine. I may not always be pretty but I **am** real. I may not always be politically correct but I **am** me. I may say and do stupid things but that's okay. I'm human and I will make mistakes. I won't hide my humanness nor will I pretend I've mastered it.

You see, the mere fact that we are human says we will fall short. I'll never be able to overcome that fact, no matter how hard I try. I am who I am and I will fall short. I will look dumb. I will say stupid things. I will make mistakes. I will hurt others. I will have bad hair days. I will burn dinner. I will forget important things. I will be human and that is exactly what I am supposed to be.

The fact that I let it all hang out bothers other people. I don't hide or pretend to be anything I'm not. I tend to "just be" no matter where I am or who I am with. My mother always told me she liked that because she never had to guess what I was thinking. I just said what I thought and moved on.

I do the same thing in my marriage. If we're having an argument, we're having an argument! I don't pretend. If others are around, I still don't pretend. We try to work it out and move on. Yet, if we're still mad, we're mad.

It's okay. All marriages, all relationships, all people have issues. We fight and do things we regret. We have times when we wish others hadn't seen into our private lives, because we're embarrassed by the behavior we display in the confines of our own home.

When we were first married I had a humbling experience. I was outside working with my flowers and I overheard the neighbors fighting. They were yelling about something and the conversation sounded heated. I was embarrassed and thought maybe I should go in. I chose not to and eventually the wife came out to do something else and when she saw me, she looked a little embarrassed. I said nothing and went on with my day. Secretly thinking, "I'm glad they don't hear us fighting."

It's a good thing I kept my thoughts quiet because not more than two days later my husband and I were arguing. During our argument I headed for the garage and on my way out I slammed the door and swore really loud. My husband was not in the garage. I was alone and in the silence I let a string of obscenities rip. And I let them rip loud! I don't like to swear. I try not too and I'm embarrassed when I fail. Yet on this occasion I thought, "I don't care. I'm mad and I want to yell." As I was walking back to the house, my neighbor saw me, sported a little grin and waved. I was busted. I was embarrassed—humbled.

We all make mistakes, get angry and express things inappropriately. I'm not any different. I'm just like my neighbors, and you are like yours. We're all imperfect. We're all mean sometimes. We don't have all the answers. We don't have perfect kids, spouses, dogs. We have ups and downs.

It's freeing to realize we're not alone or weird. It's freeing to know we're all real. We have all thought similar thoughts at one time or another. We have all failed. We have all hurt someone else. We have all had a bad hair day. It's okay. When we are okay with our humanness, we no longer have to pretend. We no longer have to try to make things look good. Things can be just what they are. If they suck, they suck. If they're good, they're good. Just know that it won't be long and the tide will turn. We'll experience the flip side, once again, and that's okay.

While I was fighting with my husband the other week, I ran into a friend of mine who also was fighting with her husband. We began to share our frustrations. We both wanted more romance, more intimacy, and we both felt our husbands were being insensitive. We talked and I told her how I just go "ballistic" and won't settle for anything less than I feel I deserve. I shared with her how I harp on an issue until my husband breaks down and shares with me. She started cracking up. "Really," she said. "I thought I was the only one who did stuff like that." I assured her that I do it often and, though I'm not proud of how icky I can be, I know I am being real.

It's scary to be real, but it's also rewarding. We are rewarded when others say, "Wow! I never thought that about you. I thought you had it all together. Now I don't feel so alone!"

It's awesome to connect with someone in a way that's personal and affirms you both. It's a release of energy when we can be who we are and not be afraid to let our warts show.

Be genuine. We are going to fail and no matter how hard we pretend, we'll get caught sooner or later. Remember, your neighbor may be watching you. And, Girlfriend, when she catches you screwing up she will not think less of you. She will think to herself, "I'm not alone."

A Computer Can't Hug Ya!

We live in a rapidly changing, technologically advanced world. Just think back 10 years ago. Ten years ago only the wealthy had computers at home, gas stations had attendants, and we did not comprehend the World Wide Web. Now we can buy gas without ever seeing the person running the store, we can shop at home for virtually everything, and we can communicate with family and friends without ever seeing or hearing the other person. We can live without ever interacting with other people. We only need to sit at our computers and find everything we need to function.

The technology of today overwhelms me and I have been having a hard time keeping up. We actually just bought a home computer; I think we were the last family in the world not to have a home computer. My kids thought we were living in the dark ages! I didn't know how to send e-mail until four months ago and I still don't comprehend the Web. It all seems plastic to me.

Everything is becoming so computer-orientated. We are removing the human element from too many things. We can do everything by computer—pay bills, shop, send cards, even store our family photos. Pretty soon we'll never have to leave our homes. We'll be able to live by clicking. These advances are supposed to simplify our lives, yet I wonder— are we progressing or regressing? Are we simplifying or complicating? Have we opened a world that reaches far beyond where we should even go? I wonder!

Much of the new technology has made our life easier. It's awesome to be able to send a fax or e-mail to a long-distance friend. Yet how personal is e-mail? How can we be real? How do we experience the feeling behind what the other person is saying? How much is lost in translation? Do we really touch another? I think it takes a lot less time to call someone to say hi than it does to type an e-mail. We can say hello in half the time it takes to write it.

E-mail is impersonal. It takes less of ourselves. E-mail is fine for quick communications, but it cannot replace human time. We need to look at the person we are talking to and acknowledge her. We need to touch our friends when they are hurting and smile at them when they are rejoicing, to hug them when they are crying.

We need human contact. A computer cannot hug you or look into your eyes. Only another person can touch our soul.

Let technology make your life easier if you choose, but don't get so wrapped up in it that you lose touch with the most important things in life—other people! No matter how advanced we become, we cannot live without people. We need them and they need us. I need you, Girlfriend! A computer can never replace the gift we have in one another!

Lonely in a Room Full of People

There have been times in my life when I have felt depressed. And with this depression came loneliness. I felt alone no matter who was around and no matter what I was doing. I could walk into a room full of people and still feel alone. I was out of sorts and nothing felt right. For some reason, still unknown to me, I just couldn't seem to connect with anyone. Things weren't clicking in my life. I just wanted everyone to go away. It was painful for me to be with people. I wanted to isolate myself.

Whenever I have these low times, I avoid other people. I tend to hole up with my notebook and check in with myself. I used to run to therapy every time this happened, but today my notebook is my counselor. I haven't been clinically depressed and yet I have struggled with low times. *[If you are experiencing depression that goes beyond a few low days, please seek professional help.]* On my low days it's as if a big black cloud moved in and landed on top of me. I used to let it smother me, immobilize me. I couldn't function and I couldn't move. I became stuck.

Not anymore! Now I push it out of the way. It doesn't always move easily but I've learned it will move. I'm not the only one in the world who gets the privilege of this massive dark thing moving into my life. It's more common than we think.

I think as women we tend to struggle with the cloud and yet we don't want to talk about it. We're afraid we'll appear defective or less than the rest of the population if we talk about it. We're not. We are simply human and we're not alone. We all struggle. Even the most positive of persons struggles and has low days!

The cloud bears no thought to whether you are rich, beautiful or healthy. We all experience low feelings. It's part of life. I encourage you to accept the cloud as part of life. Should you accept it and give it permission to stay? No! You accept that it exists but you don't have to let it settle in your backyard. It doesn't belong there, and we must work hard to move it out.

I said low feelings were normal and that we all experience them, yet how long we must endure them has to do with how long we allow them to stay.

Tragic things happen. We cannot stop that. Tragedy, loss, relationships and life hurt. We are going to experience pain. It's normal and no matter who you are you will experience it. You'll get hurt and grieve. It's normal and good to let grief out.

I think that honestly dealing with our feelings is one key to moving the cloud along faster. Will it go away simply because you shared it? Probably not! But you are one step closer to it moving it on.

When I have low times, I do a few basic things. First of all, I journal. I journal to find out what's going on in my heart. As I journal, I pray and ask God to help me, to show me the way through this. I think of going *through* it and not *around* it. If I go around it, I will run right smack into it again and, sooner or later, I must deal with it.

While spending time with my notebook, I list anything that's bothering me and I decide if there's anything I need to do. Do I need to share feelings with someone? Do I need to set a boundary? What do I need to do to take care of myself?

I will journal as much as I need to during the time the cloud rests in my life. I take time and I'm gentle with myself. Being gentle creates the space I need to persevere. I set aside time for a bath, a good book and a truffle. I pamper myself and trust I will get through this dark time, and I will be okay.

I force myself to move the cloud along faster by taking care of *me*. When I feel low, I make an absolute priority of exercising daily, eating healthy, getting eight-plus hours of sleep each night, getting out in the sun and cutting back on caffeine. I stop, drop and roll. I stop what I'm doing. I stop the crazy schedule. And I stop pretending the cloud isn't there. I drop. I drop expectations, duties and feelings. Then I roll. I let the course of whatever I'm going through roll away and I do what I can to make the process easier. I take care of me and let life roll on. I can't stop it even if I try, but I can make the pain in life more bearable by taking good care of myself.

I don't want to be depressed. I don't want to be lonely in a room full of people. But you know what? Sometimes I am low and I do feel lonely. I feel pain and I just want to cry. It's a scary place to be and yet I've come to realize that it's not so unusual. I can feel depressed and feel alone and I will not die. I will live through it and the black clouds will pass. Tomorrow is a new day and next week is a new week.

Girlfriend, I encourage you to be gentle with yourself in these times. Long ago someone told me that the depths of pain and despair I experienced would be the heights of joy and possibility available to me. I believe this. I know the passion for life that I have today comes from knowing what's in the pit. Girlfriend, don't be paralyzed by the black clouds. They will only make the heights more beautiful!

Let's Have Coffee

My favorite time of day is that first cup of coffee. I think about it before I go to bed and I look forward to morning. I truly enjoy the first cup of the day. I love the smell, the flavor and the experience of holding the cup in my hands. I have a special kind of cream. I grind my own beans. I have a few special cups. I just love coffee. The whole experience brightens my day.

Actually the pleasure starts the night before. I prepare the coffee pot at night so when I open my eyes, my coffee is ready. As I stand at the counter grinding the beans before I go to sleep, I inhale the wonderful aroma. I absolutely love the smell and I look forward to that first cup the following morning.

There is nothing worse than waking up and finding out I have no coffee or that I am out of my favorite cream. I have been known to go to the store at midnight just to ensure that I have my supplies. I usually bring my own coffee and cream when I travel, but on occasion I forget. Then I'm crabby. I have to get up, get dressed and head out to find a good coffee shop. Or I have to brave the hotel coffee. Either way it's not the same. They never have my cream and the coffee just isn't the same. It's not a good experience. I miss my home. I miss the experience I create for myself as I wake up each day.

I have a routine that brings joy to my morning. It's simple and yet it allows me to start my day with a positive outlook and a treat for myself.

I have been blessed with a wonderful husband. He loves to bring joy to my life. He knows how much I love that first cup of coffee and he goes out of his way each day to make sure he participates. He brings my first cup to me in bed. He knows when I want to wake up and he brings me a hot cup with just the right amount of cream and says, "Here you go, Lover." It's awesome. I wake up and, even if I'm tired, I know it will be a good day. I kiss him and off to work he goes. Then I'm alone in the silence of the morning enjoying my coffee. I plan my day, spend some time in prayer and sip my wonderful coffee. There is no place in the world that I would rather be at that moment than sitting alone in my bed. I often get my best ideas while I'm sitting writing in my journal. Eventually I have to get up and get a refill. I shuffle into the kitchen and pour a second cup, but the second never compares to the first.

So what's up with all this talk about coffee, you ask? It actually has nothing to do with coffee. It has everything to do with creating routines for yourself that make your days worth living, creating routines that you can't wait to get out of bed for. Maybe for you, your special time comes at night. Therefore, you can't wait for evening to come. Choose a time that works for you. I love the morning simply because I start my day in a spectacular way each and every day. It helps me center myself. I face the day with energy and a strong mental attitude. But any time of the day can be your "coffee time."

What do you really enjoy? What do you look forward to? Do you love a certain kind of cereal, a certain radio station, a glass of iced tea? Whatever it is, find it! Find a time and activity that you truly enjoy. Keep it simple, something you can do each day for 10 minutes, and then do it every day. Find something you look forward to or it won't happen.

If you want to take a walk every morning, that's great. But only do it if you really like to walk and then let go of the fitness expectations. You need to want to go. I exercise every day but I don't always look forward to it. In fact, sometimes I downright hate it. I would not jump out of bed to exercise, but I would jump out of bed for my first cup of coffee. You see the difference? Find something that brings you and you alone pleasure.

Be good to yourself. Treat yourself as you deserve. Let your own "coffee time" brighten your day. Let it bring a moment of silence to your soul. We all need a breather in this crazy world and often 10 minutes can make the difference. So Girlfriend, let's have "coffee time." I know you will never go without it once you start. It's truly addicting.

Competition—We Are Not Out to Win!

Comparing ourselves to other women is a dangerous mental game. It destroys our relationships, fuels jealousy and creates deeper insecurities in our own lives. Yet time and again we choose to pick up our pieces and play the game. We all participate in some form or another and that is what fuels the competition.

The game is played like this. We walk into a crowd and we start comparing ourselves to every other woman in the room. We begin the judging process. We decide in our head who is thinner, who is prettier, and who has more than we do.

Then we measure ourselves against the other women. We develop a sort of pecking order, placing ourselves somewhere on the scale. Usually it goes like this—"I'm glad I'm not her," Wow! I wish I looked like her," "She's got a better body than

I do" or "Do I look that bad?" The thoughts spiral until we are either better than or less than every other woman in the room. This mental judging can go on for minutes or for a whole evening. We obsess about others, about what they have or how they look.

We tend to compare because we want to be okay. We want to win. We want to fit in. Many times we not only want to fit in—we secretly want to be "better than" those around us. We're insecure and we become competitive. When we do this, we lose our connections with people.

When we tear one another down by comparing and competing, we draw dividing lines. We alienate ourselves. We create loneliness and we hurt others and ourselves. We do not win.

You've all had conversations where you walk away and feel about 2 inches high. You wonder how you could ever compare to this person? She's awesome! She has an incredibly romantic marriage, the valedictorians of tomorrow for children, she's a size five (and she constantly tells you she just isn't ever hungry), and, best of all, she never lets you get in a word because she's so wrapped up in herself. When you finally do get in a word, she looks at you as if you're stupid and says, "Oh, really." You feel stupid and wish you had kept your mouth shut.

We've all been competitive and jealous, thinking things like, "I can't wait to show so-and-so my new outfit. She is going to die with jealousy." And we've been on the other side as well. We want what our girlfriends have and we silently steal their joy. We lose both ways. We lose whether we are trying to build ourselves up falsely or whether we are trying to defend what we have.

I see many of us competing and destroying relationships. It's absurd. We are grown women! In grade school, we compared dolls and in high school we compared boyfriends. It's sad that it continues today.

Many of us have grown past this, thank God! It's truly a gift to be content with your life and to be genuinely happy for the success of others. That's who I want to be. I want to live and be who I am! I want to be free to watch you live and love you for who you are. I want to encourage you, to build you up. You are valuable and you have much to teach me. We are playing a game of the heart and in matters of the heart there are no winners. Because, you see, if I win you lose.

Instead of a football game, imagine we are on a trail ride. We each go our own way. We each see different things. Some of us visit the mountaintops while others visit the desert. Yet when we come back together, we have so much to share. We learn and grow from one another. We're not all meant to go on the same ride. Our different journeys enrich our lives and the lives of those around us.

We'll all struggle with jealousy. It's a part of life. Yet it's not the jealousy itself that matters—it's what we do with it that counts. If we're careful and don't want to damage others with this jealousy beast, we'll let it roar somewhere other than at our girlfriends. Try putting it in your journal and taking a look at it there.

Is what she has something you really want? If it is, then you need to find a way to make it happen in your life. If it really isn't, then you should let it go and be happy for her. You can participate through her. Let her excitement be exciting for you as well. There is something incredibly rewarding about cheering on someone else and being excited for their success.

We often feel that if we are not happy, then no one deserves to be happy. That's a misconception. A lie. If one person being miserable means we all have to be miserable, our world is going to be a very sad place. We need happy people to build us up when we are down.

Happy people give us hope when we are sad, even if we don't admit it at the time. Rich people push us to work harder because they let us know it can be done. Beautiful people are a joy to watch. While we may never look like them, their presence can help us take better care of our own bodies. The brains of the world challenge us to think more and go farther.

Without each of the women mentioned above, our world could not function. We all have abilities to be what we are. Yours may not seem as glamorous as your neighbor's, but it's what you have. You can either use it to its fullest and walk in contentment, or you can continue to wish upon your neighbor's star.

We are definitely strange creatures, Girlfriend! We will do ourselves a huge favor if we learn how to turn away from competition. It only makes our life miserable and keeps us distant from others. We can never win the game because someone will always be better. So let's stop it right now—and just enjoy the trail ride.

Our Families

Be Silly

We have this intense fantasy that other people really care about what we do or that they are actually watching us to see if we look stupid. For one thing—who cares if they are? For another—think about how often you really have time to analyze what someone else is doing.

But when it comes to being silly or letting go, we just can't do it. What would people think? How would I look? I could never do that? So we don't! We don't laugh, we don't cry out loud, we don't rejoice, and we don't let ourselves be **silly**.

I am saddened by the innocence our children are losing at a very young age, and I'm even sadder that as adults we have little or none left. You see, innocence allows us to be goofy. It allows us moments of complete and utter childishness. It's a fresh breeze that blows into our children's hearts, and they are totally captivated by the experience and allow their whole being to participate. It's truly miraculous to watch children giggle until they cry or to watch them wrapped up in a world full of make-believe.

We need more make-believe in our lives. We need more letting-go time and more silly time. We are much too rigid, way too uptight. We are stunting our growth.

It's impossible to be in control all of the time. It requires too much energy and too much false pretense. The world is full of people "in control." You know that somewhere inside they are real, but you really have no idea who they are. They cover up with proper behavior and choose their words carefully. It doesn't take me long to become bored with these people because they are plastic. Their lives bring no joy to others. They are too wrapped up being in control to let others see who they really are. They think this makes them appear successful. But since when does being successful mean that you are stuffy and cold to other people? I define success as making a positive impact on the lives of those around me. That is true success. I believe that to cry with someone or to make someone laugh is divine success.

Let go. Be silly. Do something totally out of the ordinary! Let your imagination flow. I had an experience a few months ago with my children that truly inspired me to be silly. We were all on the trampoline, jumping and having fun. But it was hard for us all to jump at the same time because the tramp was just not big enough. I was in an exceptionally squirrelly mood, so I began to be goofy. I became an animal and everyone had to be the same animal. We crawled around the tramp imitating one animal and then someone would say a new animal and we would all become that animal. It was a blast! We were laughing, snorting, growling, and letting go. We let our imaginations come alive. To onlookers we may have looked foolish, but I didn't care. I was creating memories for my children and, more than that, I was letting go.

After an hour of being wild beasts, we collapsed, exhausted but thoroughly content! It was truly a gift—a time totally devoted to being silly and laughing together.

Another thing we love to do is dance. We turn up the music real loud and just let loose. We dance and sing and laugh. I have taught my kids to play an awesome air guitar!

I think if we took more time to let ourselves be silly, we would feel better, be sick less often and have more energy. I'm not encouraging you to go out and break the law or to break down socially accepted behaviors. I'm encouraging you to be more open to times when you can let go and participate in the silly or imaginary things in life. The opportunities are waiting for you. I can hear the laughter already. Are you going to join the fun?

Time Out

"That's it. I've had it. Go to your room for a time out."

Sound familiar? Off they go and as they leave we think, "Yes, go. You need a time out."

There are times in our children's lives when they need a time out. Sometimes they need them daily. They need to go away and ponder what it is they are doing. They need to be made aware of the wrong they have committed. They need time to reflect on what they would have done differently. A time out gives them time to diffuse their emotions and lets them get away from Mom, who is angry and needs space just as much as they do.

Just as a child needs a "time out" to deal more effectively with life, I think adults can benefit from a time out as well. Go ahead. Go to your room, lock the door and give yourself a time out. You may laugh at the suggestion, but I think many of us already resort to the bathroom or the bedroom when we're angry or hurt by someone we love. This type of time out often comes from someone else's behavior. We retreat to let the blow of emotion soften. Once we have cooled down, we can go back and make the best use of our words with the other person. This time away to cool off will keep us from turning right back around and stabbing that person with our words. I call this type of time out the "retreat time." We are retreating from something or someone to gain greater perspective on the situation at hand.

The other type of time out is harder to follow, but I think it's the one that will produce results in your life. This is a self-inflicted time out, a time out that allows you time to deal with you. We all know when we are on a roll. It doesn't matter what anyone does. We are angry; we are on the edge. It's that time of the month and everyone else better watch out because we're in a bad mood. At times like these, we need to stop and say "time out!" Then we need to go away for a little while and reflect.

And while we're reflecting, we need to ask ourselves some tough questions. Why am I acting like Ivan the Terrible? What am I accomplishing with this behavior? Do I mean the words I'm saying? What could make my present reality better?

Sometimes we will realize that we are just having a bad day. That's okay! It's days like these when we need to just take a hot bath and crawl into bed. If that's the case, then let those around you know that your mood has nothing to do with them, and then go take care of *you*!

If you experience time outs when you know you are at fault and you have no real issues with anyone but yourself, then use this time to work up the courage to apologize, and then dig deep within to change your behavior. You may not feel better that day but at least you can make a commitment to stop doing whatever it was that led you to being in the time out in the first place.

It takes courage to look within and ask ourselves why we are acting a certain way and what it's accomplishing. We may not like the answers we find but they should spur us on toward growth.

Sometimes during your self-inflicted time out, you may realize it was something at work or with a friend or some other unresolved issue that was causing you to feel prickly. If you discover this, you are blessed and you can go out and apologize to your loved ones. But you still need to deal with the source of your frustration because, if you don't, it will fester and you will find yourself prickly again tomorrow.

Admitting that someone is making you miserable or agitated is one thing, but it is more important to resolve the issue to the best of your ability. If the issue cannot be resolved immediately or completely—but you have done your part—then you need the grace to let go and move on. There have been many situations in my life where others took advantage of me and were unwilling to look at the devastation they caused. Therefore, I was left with a decision: either I could be angry forever and allow this person control in my emotional life, or I could let go and forgive, knowing that this decision would bring peace and it would set me free. Forgiveness does not excuse the other person but it makes life a whole lot more enjoyable.

I had a time out today and it was good! I went to my room and I was able to sort out the irritations I was feeling toward my oldest child. I was yelling at him for something that had nothing to do with him. It was inappropriate and I knew it.

When I said "time out" and went away for a while, I was able to put the issue into perspective, apologize for my behavior and seek out time with my husband because that was where the real problem was. When we are in the middle of something, it's amazing how out of whack things can become. Given some space, however, things that once seemed overwhelming—even devastating—become less monstrous, and we feel more able to deal with them.

By continuing to monitor your own behavior, you are in control of who you become. By giving yourself a time out, you give yourself the gift of self-reflection and you open the door to growth. You become more aware of the influence you have on others' lives. Make sure you leave a positive impression. And when you're not leaving a positive impression or are being prickly, it is okay to say, "Time out!"

It will always be okay to take a time out, no matter what age you are. We will never outgrow it but, if we're willing, we can grow from it!

I Missed It

Last weekend was Halloween. We had plans to have my family over to go trick or treating. We planned to have dinner then my husband and I were going to take the little ones out while the rest of them passed out candy.

It was going to be a very casual evening. I bought pizzas and pop. It was to be very simple. It was kind of a last-minute thing and I was really looking forward to it. Yet about an hour before they came I went into "mega work" mode. I tell myself every time that I'm not going to do it and yet, without fail, an hour or so before we are to have company I freak out.

I hate it! I always struggle with what to do differently. I lay in bed that evening after everyone left and went over the evening in my head. I had planned too many things for the afternoon and I didn't get them all done in time. So by the time it came to get costumes on and dinner ready, I was behind schedule. Yet that really has nothing to do with it, because even when I'm ready two hours before company comes, I still freak out!

It's as if something takes over my mind and declares that EVERYTHING MUST BE PERFECT! Then I take that thought and I'm off. I race ahead 200 miles an hour. I work like a dog, treat my family worse than the dog and freak out. I want everything to be perfect. I go over the house 20 times, check and recheck the food and I tell everyone not to touch ANYTHING. I put myself into an absolute tizzy fit.

Then anger takes over. I become angry at my husband because usually 10 minutes before we are to have company he is either in the shower or pulling out the refrigerator to quick clean behind it. You see he either takes care of his own personal hygiene or does something that absolutely does not need to be done before the guests arrive. He takes offense at my mood and becomes defensive. In his eyes he is helping. Pretty soon we have a major battle on our hands.

I'm pissed and he shuts down. And this makes me angrier. Doesn't he know we have to work it out? Our company will be here in 10 minutes.

So I continue dashing around the house, ignoring hubby (two can play his game), threatening to cancel the evening, yelling at the kids and fueling the bonfire that's raging in me. It gets out of control. The more I try to control it, the wilder it gets.

Then the moment arrives. They are at the door. We all look at each other and no one goes for the door. The kids don't want to answer it. I think they're afraid that we will continue our stupid behavior and embarrass them. I think they also feel sorry for the guests.

Someone eventually opens the door, we immediately put on our friendly hosting faces, and the evening begins. But inside I'm dying and feeling guilty. How could I have been so stupid? Why did I get so worked up? Why did I care if everything was perfect? They have only been there for five minutes now and the place is already trashed. What's the point? I feel bad and I know in my heart that what's important is not how our home looks or how the food tastes. It's the people who are here and the relationship we have with one another that counts. So why do I continue to sabotage the preparations and harm my family in the process?

Here it was Halloween and once again I had gone ballistic. It was supposed to be a simple affair. Nothing fancy, just pizza and trick or treating. Yet it happened again. I went into mega work mode and I wrecked the preparations once again. I couldn't get the costumes to look right, the oven wasn't turned on, and it was getting late. I began yelling at the kids who just became more defiant in my nasty mood and I launched full force into fighting with my husband. It was miserable and embarrassing. I couldn't get it under control and my teenage brother was there through all of it. I felt ashamed.

I continued to rant and rave and yell at everyone about everything. You see, in my mind, everything was someone else's fault. Nothing was my fault. I was the only one working and I was the only one who knew how it all needed to be done. Therefore, it wasn't my fault. Yet later I knew it was my fault. I had fueled the fire once again.

When my sister arrived, I was crabby and feeling bad. I couldn't shake the irritability I felt and everyone knew it. I scurried around making dinner and getting the kids to stop playing with their costumes. They just didn't get it and I was getting madder by the moment.

During dinner I half-heartedly tried to apologize to my husband who, by this point, was too mad to accept my apology. He knew I had made a mess of the evening and he had every right to be angry. He did finally lighten up and we left. We had a great time trick or treating but when we came back home it started all over again. The house was a mess. There were people everywhere and it drove me nuts. Instead of just enjoying my company I began picking up and putting things away. They left and I spent the next hour getting everything back in order. By the time it was all put away, I felt miserable. I had done it again. I had missed it.

I had missed the fun and I had missed entering into relationships with those I love. I had been so caught up in doing and preparing that I forgot to enjoy. I had missed the event. It was over and there was no way to get it back. I felt humiliated and stupid. Why did I continue to act this way? Why couldn't I just enjoy life? I lay in bed going over and over in my mind how to do it differently. I've done it a thousand times and I still do it. I miss the event. I miss the people and I miss allowing myself the gift of letting go and enjoying life.

Girlfriend, I don't know how to do it differently, but I'm learning. Each time it happens I spend more time afterward thinking it over and I feel I'm beginning to see the real me. I see how hard it is for me to let go. I have willed myself to change, prayed for the strength to change but, time and again, I have failed. Through repeated failure I have learned. And I will continue to learn and pray. I have even begun to let others in on the insanity so they can help hold me accountable.

I feel that many of our issues are like this. They become a pattern and we continue the craziness and then feel guilty. We need each other and we need to let others know where our weak points are. I'm not perfect but I'm willing to grow. And that is all I can do. I leave the rest up to God and ask Him to guide me through yet one more issue in my life. I'm also asking each of you to come along with me. We all need help and we all have areas that need work. I have mine and you have yours.

I encourage you to press on. We will experience growth, not always in the time frame we want, but it will come. And then we can look back and say, "I got it. I didn't miss it this time. I enjoyed the moment!"

Be Spontaneous

The best family vacation we ever took was planned in 36 hours. Some friends had a cabin in Colorado and called to say their cabin was open. We could use it but we'd have to leave in a day and a half. Did we want to go?

No way, I told myself. You cannot plan a vacation in 36 measly hours—absolutely not! In order to plan a vacation, you need months. You need to discuss where you want to go, how you will get there and where you will stay. The details are overwhelming. After this initial planning, you need to shop.

Shopping is essential. You need new clothes, 10 new swimsuits, $20 worth of magazines, suntan lotions of every kind and variety, a new novel, beauty supplies in small sizes, treats for my purse and, of course, new luggage.

Then there are the kids. You need tons of travel supplies, treats for a year, two outfits for each day, new sunglasses (better buy two because the first ones will get lost before you leave the house), new small toys (so they won't be bored), batteries of every type for all their electronic gadgets, and they always really need one more thing.

The shopping requires weeks. There is no way to do it in less than 36 hours. Once the shopping is done, you move on to packing.

Packing is an art form. I usually start three weeks ahead of time. You need to create a good list. Then you may have some more shopping to do. There's always something on your list that you don't have at home. Once the list is created you can actually gather the luggage and the storage containers for your stuff.

Then the ironing, sorting and outfit matching begins. You go through each drawer and decide what goes with what, when you will wear each piece and how it will hold up in the suitcase. This takes time—I mean real time—it cannot be done in less than 36 hours.

When the packing is done, you review your list. Did you forget anything? Are you going to need that other pair of sandals? Yeah, you better throw them in, just in case. Heaven forbid you'd be without something you really need.

Then comes the waiting and the anticipation. That's the fun part. You lose sleep because you are so excited. You can't wait to go. You cannot build up to a vacation in just 36 hours. A vacation is a process and that process requires time and energy. Usually by the time I leave for a vacation I'm exhausted and actually need a vacation.

Well, we decided to go on this trip, against my better judgment. I figured this would be an adventure and maybe—just maybe—I'd learn something. I let go of my usual vacation routine and decided to just do it! We threw a few things in the van, fueled up and off we went. We had three kids in tow and a few outfits in a suitcase. We had no treats or new toys for the car. I didn't have 10 new swimsuits or a stack of magazines to read by the pool. Yet we had what was most important—we had each other. We were spending time together.

All of a sudden, the planning didn't seem so important. We were vacationing. We were on an adventure. We had no idea where we were going, we didn't know where we'd stay along the way, but we were doing it. We sang and laughed and stopped for treats. We had to actually stop and enjoy new places for treats because we didn't buy them ahead of time. The kids had never been so good in the car. I was shocked. I felt relaxed, I wasn't worried about what we forgot and I didn't care. It was strange; this was unlike me, yet I really liked it. We traveled on. We had no expectations of what we would find, but we knew we were going to have fun.

Well, fun was exactly what we had! It was the best vacation we ever had. Was it because the place was perfect? No! Was it because I had all the latest swimsuits? No! It was because we let go and decided to be spontaneous. We decided to try something new and not worry about the details. We just went and had a blast! Looking back on that vacation, I realize I learned a lot about myself.

I learned that being spontaneous simplifies life. I get so caught up in the details that I miss the simple joys. I learned that it's okay to just go. I learned I liked being adventurous, that being spontaneous lightened my soul and brought a childlike freedom. I liked being stress-free and not worrying about every little detail. I let go and enjoyed myself. My family enjoyed each other and we had more fun than we'd ever had before. We had no agenda, no expectations and no preconceived ideas. We just went!

Spontaneity diffuses controlling behavior, it overcomes boredom, and it gives you a new lease on life. As I look over the last year of my life, the best moments I had were moments of spontaneity. Lack of spontaneity stifles your creativity and it will snuff out your fire. My passion for life comes alive as I let myself follow the rainbow just to see where it leads. My fire is relit when I take time to go out and look at the stars. My inner being is at peace when I decide to enter into a spontaneous water fight with my children. Life is short, work is hard, and stress is all around us. We must carve out times to just go with it.

You can just go, too! You can go on a mini vacation, go for dinner somewhere new or go for a midnight swim. Just do something on the spur of the moment. Look for opportunities to be spontaneous and then jump on them. Don't miss out. There's much adventure waiting to be experienced. You'll experience life in a new way. Let's go, Girlfriend—let's find out what life has to offer when we're willing to grab it as it comes.

I Didn't Just Want to Run Away From Home—I Did!

A few years ago, I had had it. I've had it many times since then, too, but this time I had really had it! I just couldn't take it anymore. My kids were driving me crazy, I was fighting with my husband, the bills were too big, the stress was too much, and I just couldn't take it anymore. I blew. I was so angry that every swear word I could possibly think of was ready to come flying out. I was absolutely berserk!

I had been home-schooling our oldest, chasing a preschooler, holding a crying baby and fed up with the whole marriage thing. Life was not fun and I just wanted to get in the car and never come back. I felt insanely guilty for even thinking those thoughts, yet that's how I felt. Life was just too much. I wanted to leave it all behind. I felt as if I had given all I could give and now I was going to blow up!

My mother happened to call in the middle of my insanity and I burst into tears. I told her I needed to get out of here and I needed to go now! She actually encouraged me to go. She told me to find somewhere to go and that she would be there in 10 minutes to stay with the kids. She said, "Just get ready and don't worry about a thing." I think she was afraid for the safety of her grandkids. She had to save them from this raging lunatic of a mother! In all reality I think she encouraged me because she knew I needed a break!

I packed frantically, told the kids and called my husband to say I was leaving and my mom would have the kids. He immediately panicked. We had been fighting for days, so he thought I was leaving him. I assured him I was not leaving the marriage but that I was getting away for a couple of days. He encouraged me and assured me he loved me.

Wow! This was easy. I was actually feeling better already. After packing, I called a local retreat center and booked a "hermitage" for the next two days. I was off and it felt great.

As I pulled out of the driveway I began to sob. I cried so hard I thought I would run off the road. I was miserable for a while but the longer I drove, the more relaxed I felt. I stopped at the store, bought all my favorite treats and took off again. I felt free, I felt young, and I felt a much-needed sense that I was still Michelle. I needed some time for me. I assured myself that I would be okay again.

I pulled into the retreat center and again the tears started to flow. I'd never been here before, but I'd heard about the place from many of my friends. I would be alone in a cabin in the woods for two whole days. I'd be without indoor plumbing, without electricity and without other people. I'd be alone with God.

After the guide left, the silence was overwhelming. It was SO quiet. There was not a sound in the cabin and it was getting dark. I am terrified of the dark, or at least of being alone in the dark. I panicked. "What was I doing here? I couldn't possibly stay here alone. What was I thinking?" Yet there I was in the middle of the woods where creatures lived, and I was alone, and it would be dark soon. I just about went home. I was so upset when I left that I hadn't even thought about the fact that, being here, I would have to face my worst fear in the whole world—being alone in the dark!

Now I was really stressed. I was stressed before I came. I was stressed for months prior. I thought this would be good and now I had to stay alone in the woods for two nights. I decided I'd just stay up all night and I would sleep during the day tomorrow. That is normally what I do when my husband goes out of town. I stay up until the sun comes up and then I go to bed.

I sat down on the little twin bed to write in my journal and I began once again to cry. I sobbed and sobbed and sobbed. I cried out to God, "Where are you? Have you left me?" I was angry, confused and frustrated. I felt dead inside. I then challenged God in my anger. I told him that if He really loved me, He would let me see a deer in my window!

I thought, "Yeah, right. Who do I think I am?" You don't challenge God. You don't take spiritual things so flippantly. I felt sure I was doomed. I thought I might be struck by lightning any moment. Afraid, I just kept on writing and ignored the window completely.

After about five minutes, I felt a nudging. "Look. Look out the window." I looked up and I began to cry out loud. There were three deer standing right in front of the picture window. Not one but three! I cried as I watched them. They were eating and as I watched them, they all stopped and looked up toward me. I now knew how much God loved me! He loved me more than I ever thought. I cried and watched the deer. My whole body was one big goose bump. As I write this, I again cry and my body again becomes one big goose bump.

It was a miracle. God knew I needed a miracle. He knew I needed to know His love and it took the three deer for me to believe it!

I was no longer afraid. I was no longer worried about the dark. In fact, while I had been watching the deer, it had gotten dark. It was very dark when I finally got up and turned on the lantern. Yet I felt okay. I felt relaxed and I knew I was going to be okay.

As I went to bed that night, I wrestled with fear once again, but this time it was different. I knew God was there and that I was right where I was supposed to be. I gave my fear to God and I actually drifted off to sleep. I slept for 12 hours. I had been exhausted. I had needed to sleep!

I believe we all need to run away sometimes. Running away does not always have to be a bad thing. Now, if I'd run out and had an affair or gone to the bar or deserted my family, I would have made matters worse. I would have put agony on top of defeat. That is not the type of running away I would encourage.

I find that I get so caught up in taking care of everyone else that I forget to take care of me. I get crazy with schedules and activities and I "do" until I am fried. I need to run away. Maybe it's only for a cup of coffee or maybe it's for a whole week.

Girlfriend, I encourage you to run away with yourself. Follow your heart and take time for you. If you plan ahead to regularly run away with yourself, you won't need to go in a crisis moment as I did. By doing it regularly, life will not build up and become explosive.

I now take one weekend a year and I go back to my little hermitage in the woods. It's my time to just be. I remove the distractions and let down. Sometimes I literally sleep for the first 24 hours. That's okay—I know I need it and I feel like a new person when I wake up.

Run away with yourself, Girlfriend. You need time for you!

Go Away for the Holidays

The holidays are supposed to be a joyful time. We have romantic visions of relaxing by the fire, singing Christmas carols and reminiscing about Christmases past. We long for quiet and peace and reflection.

Yet reality is often quite different. Today we are supposed to connect with others while in the midst of cookies, Christmas shopping, writing cards, entertaining, going to parties and decorating. We cram more into the month of December than we do the whole rest of the year. Each year Christmas craziness gets bigger and noisier and just "more" more.

Every year I vow that I will get off the Christmas-go-round. Every year I vow that it's going to be different. "I am going to slow down and just enjoy the lights on the Christmas tree." "I am going to sit by the fire and drink hot chocolate."

"I am going to buy less and spend more time with the ones I love." Yet I fall short every year. By the time December comes I am running nine hundred miles an hour and I miss it. When it's over, I'm exhausted, sick and crabby. I vow I will never do it again!

I have always done the Christmas-go-round. I get stressed every year and it's not fun! By the time it's over our whole family is exhausted and we all feel ripped off. We feel ripped off because we never spent any time together. My husband and I both come from families where they get together 25 times in the month of December. We have both bought into the Christmas-go-round hype and we feel there is no way we could give up one thing. We have to do them all. What would people think if we didn't come? Who'd be offended if we didn't send out cards? How could we stop buying gifts?

This is what Christmas is supposed to be. It only comes once a year and we tell ourselves that we'll live through it. We try to convince ourselves that we are having fun and that we do it for the older generation. I do agree whole-heartedly in honoring the older generation, but I don't believe this has to happen only in the month of December!

One year I had absolutely had more than I could handle and I told my husband I wanted to go away for Christmas. He couldn't believe what I was saying. "Not go to Christmas! We'd be the black sheep forever!" I continued, "I don't care. I need to do this and I want you to come with me." He agreed—reluctantly, but he agreed. Once that hurdle was over, I had to face the family. They were not as easy to satisfy. They were angry and hurt. We were breaking family law!

I found a cabin way up north and reserved it. I didn't care what it looked like as long as it had a fireplace. I sent in my money and felt like a million bucks. I was free. I was doing something I had always wanted to do but never had the guts to do. Did this mean I didn't love my family? Absolutely not! I loved them all dearly. I loved to spend time with each one of them. Yet I had my own family now, and I wanted to set Christmas traditions for the four of us. I wanted to step out and experience my "dream Christmas." I decided that if I didn't just go for it, it would always be just a dream! Off we went.

When we arrived it was dark and snowing. It was beautiful. I had brought good food, family games and the three people who meant the most to me in the whole world. I had everything I ever wanted for Christmas. Once inside our cabin, I saw the most beautiful sight in the world. The resort owners had cut down and set up a little Christmas tree for us in our cabin. It was Christmas!

We spent three days enjoying our family. We had stepped off the Christmas-go-round and it was awesome! I had always pictured Christmas like this. We sat by the fire, read books, played games, talked for hours at the table, cooked together and enjoyed getting to know each other better.

Unfortunately we had to return home too soon, but I will always carry the memories from the year we stepped off the Christmas-go-round. Will we do this every year? Probably not—we still need to spend some Christmases doing the mad dash to see everyone and do everything. Yet every few years we will go. I am thinking this might be the year to go again!

It truly meant the world to me to follow my heart. My family was drawn closer, we made awesome memories, and we look forward to going again. You can have the type of Christmas—or New Year or Thanksgiving or Hanukkah—that you always wanted. Let yourself experience the magic. Where will you go, Girlfriend? What will you do? Follow those dreams and let the expectations of others fall away.

Our Obsessions

Stop Obsessing

Why do we get so bent out of shape about things that have no importance in our lives? Not only do we take unimportant items and get bent out of shape about them, but we then obsess and waste our precious "thought life."

Obsessing can lead to major problems and can destroy relationships. I spent many years of my life trying to overcome a destructive thought life and to stop obsessing. I'm not there yet, but each day I make progress and I learn how to let go.

Thoughts are a strange thing. They come voluntarily when we choose to think about something, but they also come involuntarily. When thoughts come to us, we have a choice. Will we give these thoughts space in our head? Will we obsess about them? Or will we simply let them pass on through? If our thoughts are negative or focused on things that create stress, we will feel the negative impact. If we choose to focus on the positives, the thoughts that move us ahead in life, our thoughts will create joy. All too often we choose the path that creates pain and frustration.

I spent time with a woman recently who shared her wedding story with me, a story that touched me deeply because I admired her wisdom and maturity. The story was simple: she and her husband eloped in a tropical paradise. Was this their dream? Yes and no.

They had talked of having a big wedding with all the trimmings, and yet she was the one who said no. Interestingly enough, it wasn't due to the fact that she had dreamed of this tropical place. It wasn't due to the cost of a big wedding. It was due to the fact that she saw her own limitations.

She knew she was prone to obsess over details and to become consumed with making it all perfect. She knew she would spend so much time making sure everything was in order that she would forget to enjoy her day. The stressful details may have been the only things she remembered in years to come and she did not want that. She wanted to remember her husband and the love she felt for him on their special day. She wanted romance, not details. She wanted intimacy, not a show. She was honest with herself and she won. She would not look back with regret and see only the details that went wrong. She would look back and remember the love they shared!

How many of us miss out because we get so wrapped up in the details? We spend so much time with the preparations and the obsessive thoughts that we forget to enjoy the event we planned. This woman knew better. She knew that, given free rein at planning this large event, she would wreak havoc on the most important day of her life. So she chose to say no to the stress and say yes to her heart.

I admire this woman. She knew her limitations and she was willing to choose a different path. Did she regret it? Never! She thoroughly enjoyed her day and her new husband without all the stress of her obsessive thinking. She had won a battle with her thought life!

We can all learn from this woman's courage. We don't have to continue doing things that cause great stress just because that's how everyone does it. We can be different and, in so doing, be true to ourselves.

I tell myself time and time again that I'm not going to obsess over what my house looks like, how my clothes fit, how my lawn is mowed or what my life looks like. Yet I fail and find myself giving in once again to obsessive thinking. I can't enjoy dinner out because it costs too much. I can't let the kids paint because I just cleaned the floor. I can't enjoy my guests because I am too busy with the details. I can't enjoy life because there is too much to do!

Your situations and thoughts may be different from mine but we all do this crazy obsessing in one form or another. It's insane! If you could hear my thoughts while I'm obsessing, you would think I needed professional help.

What does your thought life look like? Are you free from obsessive thinking? If you are, you are doing something right! Pat yourself on the back. But if you also struggle with this phenomenon, then you need to step back and take a look. I think we could all justify or rationalize why we do it, but let's put that aside. Do we really want to be controlled by obsessive thinking or do we want to be free?

I want to be free. I want to be able to make a mistake and let it go. I want to be able to eat out and not feel guilty about how much we spend. I want to be able to live in my house and enjoy the people who are there, not care about the preparations.

Get the drift? We need to stop obsessing and start living fuller, more peaceful lives—lives where we leave room in our thoughts to be creative, playful and at peace with who we are.

I've found many things to be helpful in battling this type of thinking. The most important one is to recognize when you're doing it. When you catch yourself obsessing, you can laugh at how ridiculous it sounds and make a conscious decision to think about something else. You can! You may have to make that decision 20 times a day, but keep making it.

Obsessing about big things is quite different from what we're talking about here and may require professional help. I don't want to minimize big issues. Those need to be dealt with. What I'm speaking about in this chapter are the little annoyances and things that have no lasting value. I often ask myself, "Will this be important in 10 years or in 10 minutes?" If you ask yourself this question, you can then make a decision about how much time you want to invest thinking about it and if the thought requires further help.

Clear thought lives create clear-minded individuals who have room to grow and let new and exciting things into their lives. What are you waiting for? There's a whole world out there for you to experience. Quit obsessing and start living!

Business or Busyness

"I'm so busy!" We hear this every day from the people around us. We are prone to complain about how busy we are and how much we have to do. It's a disease and we're infected.

We create this insanity by constantly bringing up how busy we are. Some of us believe we are the busiest person on the whole planet and, no matter what any one says, they will never understand how busy our life is.

We know people like that. Maybe you are one of them. Somehow our life is busier than everyone else's and no one could understand our stress.

The bottom line is that no matter how busy we are or how much stress we have in our lives, talking about it constantly is only going to make it worse. In his book *Don't Sweat the Small Stuff*, Richard Carlson challenges us to stop telling ourselves or anyone else how busy we are—no matter how true it may be. At first I thought, "Oh, that wouldn't really work." But it did. I actually felt more relaxed, like I had more time to get things accomplished. I think the key was I stopped focusing on how busy I was and got down to business. I stopped wasting time talking about being so busy and I stopped feeling sorry for myself.

I also became aware of how many people constantly respond to the question of how they are with "I'm so busy!" Then they proceed to tell you every negative, stressful thing that is going on in their lives. Before you know it, even if you weren't stressed before the conversation, you are now!

The power of our focus not only affects us, but it affects those around us. We can either bring light and life or death and negativity. When we constantly concentrate on how busy we are, we create a vacuum, and it sucks the life out of us. It's amazing that as I took the time to really listen to others, I could see they were stressing themselves out. I'm in no way belittling or making light of anyone's stress, but I do feel that we often make it worse for ourselves. It's depressing to sit and listen to someone else describe how busy they are and that we wouldn't know because we do not have XYZ in our life. Even if we know what they are experiencing, it's better left unsaid because they are in the middle of their own pity party.

By stepping out of the cycle, you alienate yourself a little because you no longer have anything to say when approached about having a busy pity party. What I have chosen to do when given the "I'm so busy line" is to say I'm sorry to hear that and change the subject. If that doesn't work, I say that I really called to XYZ and then get off the phone.

It has become so irritating for me to listen to the busy pity party patter because, no matter who it is, it's all the same. We live in the year 2001—life is busy! Either we need to deal with it and move on or we stress out and have to move on anyway. Busyness is like air—it's always there and it's not going away. My grandparents cringe at the pace we keep and yet that's the way it is. We can learn to flow with it or at least not give it all of our mental energy, or we can let the negativity and thought processing that go with being constantly focused on telling others how busy we are get the best of us. If we learn that being busy is part of life, then we can just move ahead. It'll still be stressful and hectic at times but it'll be much more serene, I guarantee.

As I became aware of how much I complained about being busy, I heard the busy pity party talk all around me. I couldn't believe the amount of time we waste talking about being busy. Once I began to respond differently to my own thoughts and to not give into busy pity parties, I realized I had a choice.

I have choices about how busy I am. I can choose where I work, where I live, how many children I have and how many activities I am involved in. I can say yes or no to a million different opportunities. Many of them are positive, but I must choose. I have the power to choose what I do with each precious 24-hour period.

For so long I felt trapped by life. It was going so fast that I just wanted to get off. As I looked at the choices I was making, I realized I was having a hard time saying no. I was having an even harder time getting anything accomplished because I was constantly thinking about what else I had to do. I decided to sit down and evaluate the activities in my life. Then I made choices.

It was amazing to list the things I was involved in. I evaluated everything from my own commitments to my children's. When I looked at my kids' schedules, I found that this caused the most stress because it took the most of my time. Yet I wanted to do those things. I had some decisions to make. Would I continue to complain about the kids' stuff or would I choose to include it and set boundaries? I chose to set boundaries. They did not need to be involved in everything. I had thought it was important to let them do everything their little hearts desired. It wasn't. I don't get to do everything I want—neither should they.

Our family is a team and, as a team, we sat down and began making choices about how many activities we could fit in and what each activity would involve. Extra activities have come along where I have told the kids they could go under the agreement that I couldn't go to every event and that we would car pool. This has worked out well for our family.

I feel different about my kids' activities today because I have chosen to let them participate. That means I have chosen to commit my money, my time and my encouragement. Every time I begin to feel crabby, I remind myself that I chose to let them participate and that I'm going to participate gracefully and have fun. I have begun enjoying their activities more. I've also found time for things I enjoy.

Let's stop being busy pity partiers and start being busy life livers—living through what we have before us each day without focusing on the whole page, doing one thing at a time and then moving on. If life is still overwhelming, then it's time to take a good look at our commitments. Usually we are the cause of our own stress. Be good to yourself and learn to say no—it really does feel good.

Won't Work For Chocolate Anymore!

I believe I am addicted—to chocolate. I need it daily. It makes me feel good and it reminds me to pamper myself.

We should all be allowed to have a truffle every day! I think we'd be less stressed and we'd learn to take better care of ourselves.

For me, chocolate is pampering myself. It may be something else for you—a hot bath, a brisk walk, a cup of hot tea or a juicy apple. Whatever brings you pleasure, you should allow yourself to have, in moderation. If you are constantly caught up in denying yourself little pleasures, you'll become frustrated. And it's this frustration that can lead to binging and overindulging.

Don't deny yourself. Allow yourself treats. As we allow ourselves regular treats, we become more balanced.

I had coffee the other day with my mother. Before going to the coffee shop, we stopped and bought truffles, each picking our favorite. Once we had our coffee, we sat down to enjoy our treat. It was awesome. I had my favorite truffle, my favorite coffee and spent time chatting with one of my favorite people. Life just doesn't get any better than this. I felt pampered and relaxed. We had been window-shopping in a cute little town that afternoon and this was the perfect way to end it.

Now to many of you, my little coffee shop experience may seem trivial. Yet to me it was growth. It was huge! I had been a person who did not allow herself treats. I didn't make room in my life for leisure. I didn't allow myself things for *me*. I was a worker who felt she constantly had to produce.

I lived to work—I even worked for chocolate. If I had chocolate for a treat, I would sneak it. I would sneak it because I felt guilty. "I shouldn't eat this. I'll get fat."

I felt guilty and, therefore, I worked very hard to keep my chocolate a secret. When I did indulge I had to exercise because, heaven forbid, I could enjoy something without feeling guilty. I drove myself absolutely crazy. I never let myself enjoy the little things in life that gave me pleasure. I couldn't just sit. I had to get up and work. Even for chocolate. I had to work to hide it and then work to take it off!

My motto used to be "never go to bed or do anything fun until all the work is done." And guess what? It's never done and, therefore, I never sat. I could never just *be*.

How did I change? I changed slowly, one step at a time. My husband, who's the exact opposite of me, encouraged me and helped me to see what I was doing to myself. I took small steps and I began to put little things in my life for *me*.

This was hard. It was almost as if doing nice things for myself was a sin and by denying myself pleasure, I could secretly take pride in what a martyr I was. Yuck! I listened to my sick thoughts. Who did I think I was? Miss High and Mighty, doing and producing constantly. I thought I was somehow better and everyone else was lazy.

Everyone else wasn't lacking in the life area—I was! I was lacking in the most important area—people! I was pushing others away and failing to enjoy the life God had given me. Most of my life I hadn't lived, I merely did. I produced and I worked. I did not live.

Today I can live. I can sit down today and enjoy a truffle on a sunny Saturday afternoon just because I'm worth it. You see, I am no longer working for chocolate—I'm enjoying it!

Girlfriend, would you please enjoy a truffle with me?

I Work Like a Dog—Probably Harder Than a Dog

I don't know where the saying "work like a dog" comes from and I doubt if dogs really work that hard. Most of the dogs I see are lying around salivating, begging for love or lazily hanging out. They don't normally work up a sweat, but we still use the phrase "work like a dog." I **do** work, and I know I work much harder than a dog. I work myself right into the ground, and then I wonder why I'm tired and burned out.

Do you struggle with being a workaholic or performance-based individual? Do you work like a dog? I do. I hate to admit it to myself. And I really hate to admit it to you. I am focused on producing. And I'm sorry to say I'm not focused enough on living or just being. I keep telling myself I will learn how to slow down and I will learn how to relax but I never follow through.

I know what is good for me but doing it is something else entirely. I vow to just have coffee and sit on the front porch and yet any spare second I have is spent running around accomplishing something. I find things to do that don't even need to be done. I do and redo and do some more. I drive everyone around me crazy. I hate this fact about myself and I struggle trying to change it.

I come from a background where I could never do enough. Nothing was good enough and I tried to always do more so I could gain approval. The approval never came, and here I am—30 years old and still doing, still trying to gain approval. Who am I trying to get approval from? I don't know. I've often wondered that if I did get this approval I'm seeking, would it really matter? Am I in such a habit of just *doing* that, even if I got the approval, would I feel content? I don't think so.

Other times, I feel that my overdoing comes from an intense fear of just *being*. If I *do*, I don't have to go inward. Therefore, the busier I am, the less I have to deal with what is really on the inside. It's easier for me to stay busy around the clock than to learn to be okay with me. If I'm producing something, I have worth. If I'm sitting, I'm doing nothing and, therefore, I am not worth much. Sounds crazy doesn't it?

Yet, no matter how crazy it sounds or how far I think I've come, I still struggle with this. I can never do enough, and it's never good enough. I constantly need to do more and be more and just produce something—anything—of value. I can't stop the merry-go-round. It feels as if the ride will never stop.

So what have I done to overcome this working-like-a-dog syndrome? Well, to be honest, not a whole lot. I have meticulously arranged my garage with matching rubber totes and labels this week. I have cleaned every closet. I have organized my office five times. I have managed our hockey team and all the details for the next month. I have paid the bills for all three business accounts. I have written daily, exercised daily and been at every sporting event my kids have had. I have done 15 loads of laundry, washed out the cupboards, rearranged the bathroom shelves and cleaned the boat. I have sent out 10 letters and cards to family members, made 24 phone calls to businesses, run 17 errands and done some of my Christmas shopping. Then I came home and looked for something else that needed to be done.

This is insane. This is not living. This is nuts.

So now that I have unloaded my week, I am challenging myself to look the monster right in the eye and vow that it will conquer me no more. It may take a while, but I vow to kill this ugly thing before it kills me. I have good intentions, of course. I've had good intentions before, but this time is different. I can't take it anymore. It has to stop. I have to make it.

I took out my planner today and made a few dates with myself. These are dates where I will actually leave the house and do nothing. I go sit by the lake, have coffee or read a magazine. I will produce nothing. I am challenging myself to one date a week for a minimum of an hour. I know it seems small but I need to start somewhere. I need to overcome this monster one step at a time. If I start too large, I will become overwhelmed and give up. I don't want to lose sight of the goal—making a lifestyle change and slowly letting it become normal. I am starting small, but I know that, as I take these small steps, the results will come.

The other thing I did was to give myself a work deadline—9 p.m. That means that I may not work after 9 p.m.! This will be tough, but I am going to do it. I cannot work until midnight and then get up at 6 a.m. and start all over again. It's not healthy. I'm not setting a balanced example for my children. I'm teaching them bad habits. We all know our children learn more from our actions than from what we say. I tell my children they need rest and they need to take care of themselves, but then I don't take care of myself. That's not right. I need to do as I tell them to do.

Without taking care of myself first, I have nothing to give anyone else. And I will not be fulfilled in any area of my life. I need down time. And I need you, too. I need you to join me on this journey. I believe that if we all begin to slow down together and quit working so hard, we will actually get more accomplished than if we are constantly busy. It's in the still of the night that the revelations come. Our creative selves can take over and we will accomplish so much more if we can just learn to be.

I need you to help me be. I need you to slow down with me and to encourage me. Will you join me? Will you stop and take a look at the pace of your life and decide with me this day that you will slow down and be? I would love to spend time along this journey with you. I believe that to learn how to be is to set our souls free! Let's be, Girlfriend! Let's conquer this monster together.

Get Out of the Box

We like packages. We like them neat and pretty and in order. We think they look beautiful and we don't want them to get messy. We are careful not to crush the bow and we wrap them as beautifully as we possibly can.

Gifts are awesome. Wrapped packages are a fun thing. But too often I try to live like a beautiful package. I try to have my corners neatly tucked and I try not to ever look messy. I want to appear crisp and clean and well-packaged. I want to be in order and the box defines my boundaries clearly. You see, when I am in a package you can clearly see my boundaries and my rules, and, therefore, you best not mess with them because I'm all packaged so nice and neat!

I have struggled with this my entire life. I have always been prone to the "beautiful package syndrome." I love

Christmas and birthdays. I love the packages the best. As a little girl, I would sit on the packages. I didn't want to open them; they were way too beautiful! I enjoyed the experience of sitting on top of them. No one else could have access to my beautiful packages.

I am still like that today in many ways. I am sitting on top of my package much of the time, looking out at the world. I have it all figured out. I have my own set of rules and regulations. They make the parameters of my box and I strive to keep the outside decorated beautifully, thus hiding whatever may be going on inside. I tie a big bow on top and shout, "Hey world! Look at me." I am defined, well put together. I know the boundaries, and I look good.

Yet do I really? When I have stopped and really searched my soul, I know I do not have this thing called "life" whipped and I am not a beautifully wrapped package. I don't resemble the beautifully wrapped box with a perfect bow. You know the kind—where the corners are perfect and the package is wrapped tight. I am not that, although it is what I strive to be. I think I am much more like a gift bag—one that has been passed around the family many times. I probably had it and gave it five times myself.

I am that bag, full of the confetti-type string and lots of old crumpled tissue paper. It's rumpled, it's been used many times and is a little damaged. It is hanging open on top, and the tissue and confetti mixture is wildly spewing out. It still looks fairly good but you can tell it isn't new and that it has been used many times. Yet it is what's inside that counts, you insist. In this case, the giver's heart was not concerned with the outside but was enthralled with what was inside.

I want to be more like that. I have struggled against my own set of "shoulds" and "shouldn'ts" for way too long. I have tortured myself with a list of "how to" and "how not to." I have pushed and shoved and squeezed myself into a box that was way too small just because I thought that was what I was supposed to do. I have tried to be put together and perfectly beautiful, but it's not me. It's time for me to come out of the box. I am not a box person, and it's time to break free!

I am forcing myself to break free from my box. I have no choice. I must move on. You see, I told God I was willing to grow and that He could change me. But I didn't really want it to hurt. I wanted to stay comfortable. Inside my box, I was warm and snug. Of course it was warm—I was suffocating in there.

It was comfortable because I knew the rules and I knew the box. It kept me from the world. I had made up a list of rules in my head that I thought "good people" should follow. I kept myself so boxed in and judged others who did not fit into my box. They were out of control. How dare they act like that? Keep it together. Keep it in. Never expose your thoughts or feelings lest you be stepped on.

That was my motto and it worked well for many years.

Yet the more I shoved into the box, the fuller it became and the harder it was to keep it all in. I was trying to be someone I was not. I was trying to look like what I thought I "should" instead of just looking like me. I was miserable.

It was only when the packaging began to fall apart and the contents began to spill out that I realized how miserable I was. My life began unwrapping slowly and soon I could not stop it—nor did I want to.

I began to feel free as the packaging fell away. I could breath. The air was awesome. Yes, the process was painful but in the midst of it all there was peace. In the middle of the turmoil, I was coming out of the box and it was awesome.

I realized that I do not nor will I ever fit into a box. I am not square or round. I am the gift bag, lumpy and frumpy and wildly spewing out confetti. I knew I needed to shake off the old rules and let the tissue hang where it may. I began to see the dysfunctional set of rules that had governed my life. As I began to list them, I saw how destructive they were. No wonder I was suffocating.

I want to share my list with you. Maybe it will encourage you to make your own list and help you to break out of **your** box or whatever keeps you from being you.

My destructive "Perfect Package Syndrome" messages were:

- I should go to church every time the doors open.
- I should eat less or eat healthier.
- I should not yell or swear—ever.
- I should cook every day for my family.
- My house should be spotless.
- Good girls don't like sex.
- I should be busy every second of every day. "Produce" was my motto.

- I should exercise every day.
- I should not feel discontent.
- Good parents don't feel like running away from home once a day.
- Moms are supposed to know how to bake.
- God is watching me, waiting for me to make a mistake.
- I am defective, therefore, I must let no one know who I really am.
- I am not as good as everyone else.
- I should talk less and be more proper.
- I must look good and never tell anyone what I really think.
- My feelings are not important.
- A mother's job is to give up everything she enjoys for everyone else.
- Anger is wrong.
- I was unlovable because my own father did not love me.
- I should not feel ill feelings toward anyone.

I could go on with my list for days but I think the above list illustrates just how confining my box was. It was miserably hot, and it was stifling me. Yet it was somehow comfortable, because it was familiar and safe. It kept me stuck—yet stuck was all I had ever known.

I am living outside the box today. I am throwing off the bows and unwrapping the paper. I am cutting up the cardboard box and jumping in the confetti of life. I am on my way to being free.

I still crawl back in the box once in a while. I long for its comfort, but each time I crawl back in, I feel more uncomfortable. I have grown since leaving the box. I have grown so much that I no longer fit and now the box is more uncomfortable than ever. I try to stay for a while but then I have to leave. I have no choice. I quickly jump back into my worn gift bag and I can breath once again. The tissue is worn and the confetti never stays in one place for long. In the rumple of the bag I am me!

Girlfriend, jump out of your box! Jump into a freer and more fulfilling life. Throw off the package that binds you and allow freedom into your life. Be whatever kind of gift you were created to be!

Accept, Accept, Accept

There are things in life that are out of your control. In fact there are actually very few things in life that we can control. Our lives depend on other people and circumstances. If we looked at what we are in control of and what we just think we are in control of, I think we would be shocked at how little we actually control.

But you say, "I have control," "I control my life" or "I control those around me." I disagree. I believe you think you have control, but actually you do not.

I have been a controlling person most of my adult life. I want to do everything. I feel better when I have it all together. Or do I really? I think my controlling behavior gives me a false sense of authority and it keeps me distant from others.

Controlling keeps us from being intimate. It keeps us isolated and alone.

I'm grateful my husband has stayed with me. He's a saint to have lived with all I've put him through. I was insecure and struggling with who I was when we got married. I instantly took control of everything. He didn't object and that's how our life began. I controlled everything—the money, the social calendar, the house, the kids and the future. I was anal and often cruel. I thought I had it all figured out and, therefore, he should do everything my way. I controlled everything and got angry if he didn't toe the line. If he spent money without asking, I was furious. If he didn't consult me on a decision, I became irate. I had a storehouse full of anger and he often caught the brunt of it. I'm embarrassed by the behavior I exhibited at home. By controlling, I somehow felt secure. But it was a total fantasy. I didn't have any control—I only thought I did.

My husband (God bless him) loved me through those first years and I learned a lot. I had so many lies floating in my head. I believed that since my growing up years had been hell and that my own father had been abusive, I had to keep the lid on my own marriage or else it would be an encore performance. That was a lie! I wasn't reliving my childhood. I was married to a man who loved me and who would never hurt me. I was an adult and I had to learn to accept the past and let it go.

I was living in fear—fear that if I didn't keep it all together it would fall apart. I thought the world would literally stop if I didn't keep things under control.

The problem was I was controlling things that didn't need to be controlled. I didn't need to be my husband's mother. He was an adult, capable of making decisions, and he had a right to be himself. I'd been trying to make him into a carbon copy of me and I was pushing him away. I married him because I loved him, he had so many qualities that I wanted and I admired the strength of his character. Yet when my own fears arose, I became a control freak. I controlled how the house looked, what we ate, how we dressed, where we went, and what we did.

My life was miserable. I couldn't let down, I couldn't trust, and I couldn't let anyone else do anything for fear they wouldn't do it right. By controlling everything I was keeping my family from being a team and limiting our growth. I was the only one who could do anything right, therefore, no one else tried. It wasn't fair to any of us. The whole world was not revolving around me, nor did I have all the answers. I needed the input of my family and they needed to give it. We were a team and it was time for me to start realizing I was not the entire team.

Acceptance has been a long, slow process for me. I have had to daily accept my family for who they are. They think differently from me. They're good at different things. But we can think and act differently and still be a family. In order to win, we all have to play as a team. You see, for a long time I was trying to play for everyone, and I was exhausted. I couldn't keep up and they couldn't even get off the bench. It was unhealthy and I didn't want to live that way. I came to see that my family was a safe place to practice and to grow. I learned to accept!

I had to accept! I had to accept the fact that the floor was dirty; accept the fact that my husband loved to watch sports, even though I thought it was an incredible waste of time; accept the fact that they all had unique tastes in clothes, food and in how they kept their rooms. I had to accept the fact that my way was not always the best way and that each member had valuable input into the direction we should take. I had to accept me for who I was and to accept the fact that I was afraid. I was afraid to do the marriage thing. I was afraid of being a parent. The bottom line was I was afraid I'd screw up. So I held on too tightly and I almost smothered my family. My controlling behavior was wrapped in fear and insecurity.

I thank God my husband loved me in spite of my behavior and that he was willing to let me grow. We sought counseling, took parenting classes, went on marriage retreats and we learned new ways to communicate. No one taught me how to parent in a healthy manner. My mom just did everything. No one taught me how to be a family. We just survived. I had to decide to take responsibility for my own life and learn what I didn't know. I had to accept the fact that I had a dysfunctional past but I still had to accept responsibility for my future. It no longer mattered what happened in the past—what mattered was life today. I had to decide if I wanted to let it ruin my life or if I wanted to learn from it, to overcome the obstacles. I had to accept me and to accept life as it was right now—today!

I must confess this is an area of continual struggle for me. I am growing and I have made progress, but I have a long way to go. I still obsess about the house, I still get angry when it's not done my way and I still blow up at my family for not doing whatever I think they should. I still fall into "control freak mode." But today there is a difference. Today I catch myself. Today I am committed to stopping the craziness.

When I find myself doing the control thing, I stop, remove myself from the situation for a moment and take time to figure out what's up. Where is this coming from? I often find it comes from fear. And the fear is often related to something totally removed from the present situation. When I sort through what's going on, I calm down. I tell myself to stop. I know that when I get myself in a "tizzy," the hardest thing for me to do is stop. Yet that is what I need to do—just stop it and stop it now!

After I have had this time-out session with myself and I feel like I can actually go out and function like a nice person again, I go back to the situation at hand. I apologize and ask for forgiveness for my behavior. I may act like an idiot but I am not too proud to admit it and to ask for forgiveness. No one ever told me they were sorry. No one ever said their behavior was wrong; they just kept doing it. I may not be perfect and I'll continue to make mistakes. But I will say I am sorry!

We all fall short, we fail, and we struggle. Yet, we can say we are sorry, and we need to. We need to commit ourselves to continual growth. We need to accept our lives and accept others. Accepting others doesn't mean you agree with everything. It means you stop playing God and let people be who they are. You are free to be who you want to be but you need to remember that everyone else should have the same opportunity. They need to be who they are—not who you want them to be. Let go. Accept life as it is. It's okay to strive to be more, but it's not okay to be a "control freak." Control kills relationships. It keeps us lonely, out of control and isolated.

Girlfriend, do me a favor today. Accept one thing in your life. Choose just one. Now make a conscious decision to accept it the way it is. Let it go. Just for today. Accept, Accept, Accept!

The Joneses Aren't Happy Either!

You admire the neighbors. You want what they have. You are jealous. You dream about what life would be like if you were in their shoes.

We all do it in some form or another. We wish we had …, or we wish we looked like …, or we wish our husband or children … Or we just plain wish our whole existence could be different. But we would never tell anyone what we think. I think we are embarrassed to admit we think others have something we do not. Therefore it is easier to have secret jealousy.

We all think about things we don't say out loud. I know I do. There is a great debate that goes on in my head and the words spoken there often stay locked up inside and never get out. "I wish I had a body like that." "I wish I had a husband who did that." "I wish my past had been like that." "I want a

Dad like hers." "I want to have family time like the neighbors." "I want to be more in control like my friend Sally." "I want to have more friends like the Smiths." "I want to be a put-together woman. You know the kind—the ones who look great no matter what they're doing."

I spend time, without often even realizing what I am doing, being jealous or wishing my life were somehow different. What an absolute waste of my time and of my inner peace. Why do I do that to myself? What am I going to gain from wanting to be a different person or from being jealous? Absolutely nothing!

I'm here to tell you this jealousy wishing isn't going to change who you are. It will just make you frustrated and unhappy. You see, we can only be truly happy when we are being who we were created to be, not who someone else was created to be. You are **you** and I am **me**. That's the way it's supposed to be and we need to get over this jealous wishing.

The icing on the cake with this whole jealousy thing is that the neighbors don't have it all either. I bet if you could be a fly on the wall in their home for one day you would be shocked. You would no longer want what they have and you would return happily to your own home and be grateful for what you have.

I have witnessed countless situations where I wished I could be like so and so only to find out there is abuse in their marriage, or they had an affair, or they have an eating disorder, or they struggle with depression or some other plague haunts their daily life.

Do we know these things from the outside? Not always! Is everyone hiding a big secret? No! Yet I think we only see the good stuff in others' lives and we see the whole of our own.

When we compare the whole of our own life to just the good of someone else's we will always come up short. We are comparing apples to dog bones. It is not an equal comparison. If we are going to compare, we need all the facts and let's face it, Girlfriend—most people will not come up and say, "You know I look great on the outside but I am miserable. My husband beats me, my kids hate me, I purge myself daily, I drink to fall asleep, I've had two affairs this week, my boobs are fake, my bank account is depleted and all that you see is a lie." Most people don't walk around airing dirty laundry.

We have to compare reality to reality and most of the time we do not know the neighbors' reality. When was the last time you had friends divorce and you thought they had a marriage made in heaven?

The bottom line is that people's lives are full of things that we are not aware of. The neighbors don't have it any better than you. You just see what they want you to see and they see what you want them to see. You may desperately want to be like them, but ya know what? They may want to be like you.

We do not need to be like anyone else. We are who we are and who we are is good enough. You can never be someone else and you would not want to be, even if you were given a chance. You say, "Right, I would jump at the chance to be so and so." But I bet you would want to be yourself again as soon as you stepped foot into someone else's life.

We were not created to be someone else. You were created to be you! Being you and truly liking who you are will bring joy, contentment and peace to your life. You will be able to go farther and live fuller. You can only truly be successful when you are you. You cannot be successful being what someone else is. You are what you are, and if you don't like who you are, then you have some work to do. There are many things you can change and many people who will help you. But you have to be you!

Girlfriend, I love ya just the way ya are! Be free today. Be free of jealousy and comparisons and be who you were created to be. Just remember—the neighbors don't have it all figured out and they aren't necessarily happy either!

Ourselves

The 'No' Nightie

At times, I wear an old blue-flowered flannel nightgown. This gown covers me from head to toe. It's old and tattered. It looks like something my mother—actually my great-grandmother—would wear. I got this nightgown as a gift when I was 14 years old. It has definitely seen its better days. I have thought many times that I should throw it away but I cannot because it has become symbolic. It is symbolic because it sends my husband a message loud and clear—"NO." I don't even have to say a word; he knows. He comments, "Sure am glad you have the "no nightie" on tonight, honey!" And I say, "Yep, so am I!"

Don't get me wrong; I really do like sex. I enjoy making love to my husband. Yet there are times when I need to say no and I need to be respected for saying no. At times I need my own space and I need to be alone. I need to wear my old ugly nightgown and crawl in bed with a good book. I need space! My husband knows that he better stay out of my way when I put this nightie on.

When do I wear my "No" nightie? I wear it when I'm sick, sad or lonely. I wear it when the world is crashing in around me. I wear it on period days. I wear it when I need to be alone or when I need to just "veg" out! I wear it when I need to be okay not being okay. I wear it when I want to say "no."

Does the "no" just mean no to sex? Not on your life! It's really less about sex and more about saying no to life. It means I cannot, for the moment, take anymore input or output. It means I'm taking time out for me where there are no expectations or no relations for the moment.

It can be a 10-minute "no" or a whole evening "no." When I take "no" time, I say no to the phone, the dishes, the pile of laundry, the kids, etc. I say "no" and I take time for me. I crawl into a hot bath with my favorite book and doze. I write in my journal, have coffee on the deck and slow down. I let my mind relax.

Why would I do this? Am I weird? Do I just need a lot of time alone? I don't think either are true. I have learned that I need down time, which, for me, means being alone, being not needed for a moment and being me. It's time when I'm not a mother, a wife or a writer. I'm not a friend or a caregiver. I'm just me. It's time for restoration and refueling because life has taken its toll on me. I need to be sparked to carry on. How do I get this refreshing? By saying "NO!"

Your "no" time may go something like my last "no" night. This particular day was destined to be haywire. I awoke at 6:00 to the smell of coffee and realized I had major cramps! I wandered to the coffee pot, poured my coffee and then realized we had no cream. Not having vanilla cream for my coffee is a major catastrophe. It's not the way I want to start my day. I don't like coffee without it, yet I was too lazy to go to the store. So I settled for skim milk and a little cinnamon.

I then sat down to write for two hours. I was humming along only to be interrupted by "Mommy, I'm hungry." I get up early so that I can have time alone to write. Yet here was my precious little 4-year-old at 6:30.

I was not happy. The day was not going well. I didn't feel good, I had no cream and now I had no time to write. My train of thought was wrecked and I figured I might as well get on with my day. So off I went, making breakfast, getting kids dressed, cleaning the kitchen and doing laundry.

By 9 a.m. I was ready for my walk. As I was getting ready to leave, my daughter decided she wanted to come with me. Fine, I say, but what I didn't realize was that she wanted to wear her new in-line skates. I didn't have the heart to say no to her, so we set out only to find that she couldn't keep up.

I was frustrated at this point because when I walk, I want to **walk**. For me, it doesn't pay to be out there putting along. We were only a mile from home and she couldn't make it anymore. She was crying, falling down and begging to go home. It was a disaster. Frustrated I headed home—so much for the walk.

I got home and realized I had one hour until swimming lessons. I reminded everyone to eat something and I headed for the shower. I had an incredibly bad hair day, so I put it up and was ready to go.

I ate something while standing at the counter and then someone spilled juice all over the clean kitchen floor. I did not have time for this, I thought as I gritted my teeth and carried on.

I wiped up the spill, the phone rang three times, we couldn't find any clean towels, and we were late. "Come on, MOM. We are going to be late." "I know, I know. Get in the truck!" I yelled.

By now I felt I was going to blow. I raced frantically around, couldn't find my keys or my kids—and we were late.

I dropped them off at swimming and did 45 minutes of errands—frantically. Well, maybe that running around replaced the exercise I missed this morning.

By one o'clock I picked them up. We went home, ate lunch, did a few more household chores, answered 10 more phone calls, returned five messages, and then the hockey players arrived. It was my day to drive the car pool, and we had to fly. We were late!

I had a truck full of kids, and they wanted to jam. We were jamming, we were late, and by now I was a little crabby. I needed a good cup of coffee. Well, I had forgotten it was summer in Minnesota and, wouldn't you know, we drove right into a dead stop—road construction.

We were late and we weren't moving. "Mom, what time is our game? We are going to be late!" "I know, Sweetheart!"

I wished I had a coffee. There were no coffee shops in sight and, even if there were, I couldn't get to one because I wasn't moving.

We finally arrived at the arena. I sat at the end of the arena alone and watched the game. They lost and my son, the goalie, had a tough game. I cheered him up, gave him the old "it's not your fault speech" and off we went.

We started home—more traffic, more jamming, which means changing the radio station every two seconds because you might be missing a song on another station, and heaven only knows you wouldn't want to miss anything!

We dropped off the car pool, hurried home, threw a sandwich in our face and reloaded. We were off to soccer—late again, but we got there! Forgot the water bottle. Oh well, it was one of those days.

They lost the soccer game. We went home, made ice cream, got baths taken, got everyone tucked in, read books, said prayers, and then I headed downstairs.

I rewashed a load of laundry. The load I did that morning had sat all day and now it smelled!

I returned some more calls, paid bills, had a snack (I had forgotten to eat dinner) and finished my to-do list.

I was just about to get ready for bed when my husband came home. He had had a stressful day and wanted to unload. He wanted to sit up and talk and I could hardly keep my eyes open. I listened half-heartedly and then I said, "No, I need a time out!"

I went off to bed and just sat! I put my "no nightie" on and read my favorite magazine. I began to feel myself unwinding and was now ready to go to sleep. I rolled over and kissed my husband, telling him that tomorrow will be a better day and assuring him my time out was not because I didn't love him.

We all have days like that. They're not traumatic; they are just plain busy. We all have too much on our plates. We have too many responsibilities. We need to learn to say "no."

Will saying no make your life less busy? Probably not! But it will give you time to refresh yourself and get ready for the next crazy day. We cannot keep on giving if we don't stop and refuel our tanks. We will run out of gas and then all of our responsibilities and relationships will suffer.

Girlfriend, learn to wear your own "no nightie." Learn to stop when life is crazy and say "no." Refuel your tank and take time to discover what your "no nightie" is. Then learn to say no to life for a minute and yes to yourself! I'll even loan you my nightgown!

Let Go—Life Is Way Too Short!

We hear it everywhere—let go and let God! We hear it in self-help groups. We read it in newspapers, magazines and books. Motivational speakers preach the message, and we know it in our hearts. We need to let go! Yet have we learned how to do it? Have we really learned what it means to let go? I don't think we have!

We are living in a world where there are more fits of violence, stress-related illnesses and unhappy people than ever before. From observing the news, the schools, the workplace and the highways, I don't think we have learned to "let go" at all. In fact, I think as a society we are carrying around more baggage than ever before. Instead of letting go and letting God have control, we are taking on more than ever before. We are trying to be more, to have more and to do more. We are stressed! We are so sick and tired half the time that we can't even think straight. We carry around the stress of today, the failures of yesterday and the worries of tomorrow. Add to that issues from childhood, feelings of insecurity and other emotional baggage, and we have a time bomb waiting to explode.

In the few months that I worked in a major metro area, I was completely shocked by the amount of road rage I saw on a daily basis. It certainly has not gotten better since then either. People are irate and out of control. They freak out because someone didn't drive the way they think he/she should. They yell, scream, swear and belittle other drivers. It's scary to watch this behavior.

I believe road rage serves as a reminder that the stress in our lives today is out of control. If we are truly at peace with our lives and ourselves, we do not need to freak out at other people on the freeway. Yes, many of us drive differently, but we must share the roadways of life together. We need to let go of the stress we carry; it's affecting all areas of our lives and the lives of everyone around us.

We carry stress like a time bomb. If we don't release it or learn how to deal with it, it can kill us. Stress can consume us and literally make us ill. In addition to physical illness, stress can cause us to limit our potential. We avoid new opportunities and new creative outlets. We feel frozen and we can't handle one more new thing. Letting go of stress, anger, hurt and all the other disappointments in life will bring us more joy, and we will experience a fuller, more productive life.

I carried intense anger with me for most of my life. I was full of rage! It flared out almost every day and at everything that happened. Over the years I have learned to control it, but it still can overwhelm me. I had gone through much counseling, had lots of prayer, and yet I still struggled. It consumed me.

When I exercised, I felt a release, but most of the time I felt I was still holding it in. It began to affect my health. I would grit my teeth so hard when I was angry that it caused jaw soreness and dental problems. I ground my teeth at night, making life miserable for anyone who slept with me. As I grew older, I began having neck and shoulder problems, which I attribute to the constant stress of the emotions I was carrying.

It was painful to carry this load of emotions, yet it seemed impossible to let it go. I needed these emotions; they were my security blanket. Hanging on to my blanket meant I did not have to deal with the hurt underneath, that I did not have to feel the pain. I could hide behind my tough, hard exterior and not let anyone know how fragile I was.

By continuing to hang out under my blanket of anger I didn't have to forgive, either. To forgive was too scary; it was easier to hang on.

By hanging on to the past, I also began to hang onto everything in my daily life. The house, the car, the kids and the lawn—I wanted everything perfect and I had a hard time letting go of even the most minute detail. I'd heard it over and over again from everyone I knew, "You need to let go! It won't all cave in without you, Michelle. The world can function without you constantly worrying about it. Let go!"

I let the stress from the roadways of my life get to such a level that I developed an ulcer. I knew what this ulcer was from—it was from holding onto the anger within. It was no coincidence that every time I became angry the beast in my stomach would flair its ugly head, and I would be in pain. It was a reminder every day—let go, relax, it's not a big deal.

I would breathe deeply and reflect. Did I want to feel better? Was I willing to let go in order to do that? I decided I was.

I quit my job and began to take care of myself. I began to de-stress my life and to take a good long look at my anger. Counselors had analyzed it. They told me I was okay, that I had dealt with the issues from my past, and now I had to just walk them out.

Okay, but how was I supposed to do that? Although I didn't have a clue, I kept right on trying. I put little delights of de-stress time into my days—a coffee from my favorite coffee shop, 20 minutes with a magazine, a long bath or a brisk walk. These times were for me, time for me to de-stress and to let go, to remind myself that life is way too short to waste it on things I can't change anyway. I had to let go if I wanted abundance in my daily life and in my relationships. I just had to.

I knew I had to continue learning to let go, but I still wasn't quite sure how to do it. I looked at my friends, those who were telling me to let go, and I was surprised to find they struggled, too. They knew I needed to "let go," but they were not so good at following their own advice.

Are many of us really good at letting go? We can pretend to be but, when push comes to shove, what do we do? Do we really live out "letting go" on a daily basis? Or do we dwell on the little things, hold onto anger and fuel our emotions? Do we express our hurt, our disappointment and then move on? Are we able to let it go? I mean **really** let it go?

I still haven't mastered the true art of letting go. I am in a continual process and I probably will be forever. I remind myself daily that the little things are just that—little things—and that anger held inside will destroy me.

I also choose to practice forgiveness each and every day. Forgiveness will bring peace to your soul. We all must learn to forgive one step at a time. We will become free as we learn to forgive and move on. We have a choice to make. Will we forgive? Will we let go? Is the traffic in our life really worth getting a speeding ticket? Is it really that important? Will we let it out as road rage toward our fellow drivers?

Each day I continue to choose the road that leads to contentment and peace, a place where I can let go and let God have control of all the things that get in my way. Life is short; the roadways of life are for moving on. Let's join in and enjoy the drive.

Dream Out Loud!

That's right, you heard me. DREAM OUT LOUD! Dream big and dream loud! We **have** to overcome our fear of speaking our dreams out loud.

Why do we keep our dreams a secret? We are afraid! It's as if once we share them, they will be jinxed. Or maybe it's that once we share them out loud we will actually have to follow through and do something about them. I know this fear well for I have fallen victim to keeping my dreams locked up inside for most of my life.

As I sit here writing, I'm thinking about this book. I have only told a few safe people that I'm writing because I'm afraid. I'm afraid that if I tell people and it doesn't happen, I will look like a fool. Or if I tell people, they will want to read it and they may not like it. Or what if I write and write and write and never get anything published? Then I will have failed. At least in my own mind I will have failed! When I told my husband what I was thinking the other day, he looked at me very tenderly and said, "Honey, you cannot fail. You need to write; your book is inside of you. If your book doesn't get published, it's okay, because, in the process, you will grow and you will learn and, most of all, you will realize your greatest dream!"

To write a book has always been my dream. The thoughts for *Hey, Girlfriend!* have been swimming in my head for a long time. Yet fear has kept me from sitting down and writing it. I was afraid—afraid of failure, afraid of what people would think, afraid to share my heart, and afraid I'd waste years and never make a dime! Yet I had to decide. What was I willing to do to reach my goal? I would do whatever it took. I began to speak my dream **out loud**!

As I spoke my dream out loud, I was shocked by the support from my girlfriends. They were excited for me and they encouraged me to get going. I couldn't believe how much they believed in me and their faith in me helped me to believe in myself. I got so pumped up that I actually sat down and started writing. As I wrote, my girlfriends would call me to make sure I was still writing. They encouraged me in the process.

You see, I'd been afraid of my own dreams. My fear had kept me from moving forward and from believing I could actually publish a book that people would read. My mind couldn't comprehend the process but my heart could. In my heart, I knew I could do it and in my heart I know I will continue to write and continue to grow and that someday it will all come together. I have no doubts.

My mind causes me problems, though. It wants to doubt and discourage me and asks who I think I am. It tells me, "Look at the bookshelves. They are full of books. How do you think you will ever be among them?"

Well, if you are reading this, then I am among them and I did it! Girlfriend, it can happen. No dream is too big or too small.

Dreaming is good for the soul. Our dreams give us hope for the future. Could our world blow up tomorrow from some nuclear accident? Yes, but then we'd all be gone and it wouldn't matter. Should we stop dreaming because this may happen? Absolutely not! When we get older should we stop dreaming? No way! When we fail, should we stop dreaming? No! That's when you need to dig in and dream even harder. When you look like a fool and people laugh, should you stop then? Not on your life! People who laugh at us are jealous, because they have no dreams.

Our dreams can touch every area of our life and they can push us toward excellence. At a convention two years ago I was challenged to write down 100 things I wanted to do before I left this earth. One hundred dreams! Wow! That is way too many, I said to myself. I couldn't possibly think of that many things.

With the challenge, I was given a notebook in which to write these dreams, but I couldn't write anything. I brought the notebook home and put it aside. After a few weeks, I pulled it out and began to really think about my life and where I wanted it to go. What did I want to be? Where did I want to travel? How much money did I want to make? Who did I want to be? Who did I want to spend time with? As I began to ponder these things, I began to write and write and write.

I ended up with 135 items on my list. I was shocked; I had a lot of dreams. I read and reread the list. Then I added more.

I was excited. I had a lot to live for and a lot to accomplish. I'd better get busy.

Yet I put the list away and went on with my daily life. I used the list a few times for different speaking engagements but, other than that, it sat in my drawer. I let my husband read it and I shared a little of it with friends but, beyond that, it was just my "dream list." I had written it down. To write it was to put it in stone. I had spoken it out loud. It was final and it was mine.

Many months later I took out the list to review it. I was actually able to cross off six things. Wow! In six months I had accomplished six items on my "dream list." I was ecstatic! I was going forward and my dreams were no longer just dreams—they were accomplishments. I calculated that if I accomplished one dream a month, it would take me 11 years and four months to complete them all.

I figured that at age 27, I had a lot more than 11 years left to live, so I better get busy and dream some more. I actually did add a few and then I changed a few. You see, as we grow our dreams can change. And that's okay. That's how life works. When we grow we realize that what we *thought* we wanted, we really didn't want after all. It's not negative to realize that the dream you achieved wasn't what you really wanted. Finding out what we don't want brings us closer to discovering what we really **do** want.

Our dreams and goals should include all aspects of our life—spiritual, emotional, physical and intellectual. When many of us think of dreams, we think of material possessions. It's important that, when you dream, you include all the areas of your life. I found that by doing this, there are goals I have such as "dating my husband twice a month" that cannot be crossed off ever because they are lifelong goals. Other goals, such as spending time in prayer each day, are the same. They are ongoing. They make up who I am and guide what happens in my life on a daily basis.

It's okay to write these things down. They are goals, but they don't have to be crossed off. Living them out will give you a sense of accomplishment. Every time I read my list, I'm reminded that I'm growing and that many of the goals on my list I am living daily.

Then there are concrete dreams. The ones we can cross off forever. One of my dreams was to scuba dive in the tropics. I'd been certified in college but never had the opportunity to actually dive in the ocean. It was a lifelong dream. Well, a few years ago I did it! And it was awesome! As I went below, I began to cry (not a good thing to do 30 feet under the ocean). I couldn't believe it—I was doing something I had waited my whole life to do. I can remember watching underwater shows as a child and wishing I could be there. I spent most of my childhood wanting to be a marine biologist (until I discovered that to be a marine biologist you have to take biology).

I had an awesome sense of accomplishment that day and I enjoyed every second that I was under water.

Dreams have a way of transporting us to a new level. They allow us to feel accomplishment and they inspire us to go further, to push harder and to let good things happen to us. You need to dream, to invite success into your life and to *believe*. Good things *will* happen to you.

You will never bring good things into your life if you constantly send out the message that you don't deserve them. You do deserve them! To dream is to become all you were created to be. To dream is to lift yourself above your circumstances. To dream is to give you hope for the future and to give yourself freedom. Go on, Girlfriend. Dream, Dream, and Dream!

I believe your dreams are waiting to be acknowledged. All you have to do is open the door and claim them. Open the door, Girlfriend. An exciting new world awaits!

Be Gentle to Yourself Each Day

We work hard, play hard, think hard and are hard on ourselves. We set unrealistic expectations, plan too many events in one day and are extremely critical of every mistake we make. We take care of everyone and everything. Yet we forget to take care of ourselves. We somehow get lost in the shuffle and don't take care of **us**. We need to be gentle to ourselves each day. And we need to start today!

"Being gentle to yourself" is a process. It requires letting go and delegating things you normally do. It involves letting others do it their way. It's being kind to yourself through what you eat, how you act and the thoughts you allow in. It's the process of becoming comfortable with yourself and not allowing expectations and comparisons to dictate your life. "Being gentle" can change your life drastically.

I have been extremely hard on myself my whole life. I never felt good enough and yet—crazily—I never felt that others could do it as good as I could. It didn't make sense. I was inadequate, yet I could not handle the way anyone else did things.

People who are insecure are often controlling and can't let go. Being insecure and controlling, I ended up doing absolutely everything. By constantly doing I created tons of opportunities to beat myself up. If something went wrong, it was naturally my fault because I did everything. I set myself up to fail and to be miserable. The harder I worked, the harder I was on myself. It was a vicious cycle. I complained constantly, because I was overworked and yet I wouldn't let anyone do anything. It was crazy! I felt crazy! I could never do anything well enough and I could never get everything done. But I tried. And the harder I tried, the more I beat myself up.

I found myself mentally and physically exhausted at one point in my life, and I knew the craziness had to stop. I could not keep on. I was killing myself. I had to learn to let go, to stop working and to be gentle to myself.

This proved to be a challenge for me. I had no idea how to do it and it was uncomfortable. Yet as I learned—and continue to learn—it provided great freedom in my life. I learned I can be nice to me and I can let gentleness in. Without first being gentle with me, I cannot be gentle with thee!

How can you be gentle to yourself? Start small. Do little things for yourself.

- Sleep in when you are tired. It really is okay, and the world will not end if you do not get up.
- Eat good foods and drink more water.
- Take an hour to start a novel.
- Delegate five household chores and do not think about them again. Let go!
- Wear comfortable clothes and shoes!
- Write a list of 20 characteristics that you like about you.
- Plan a day out for yourself and do whatever you want to do.
- Get 12 hugs in one day.
- Listen to your favorite CD or tape in the car. Play it as loud as you like and sing until your little heart is content!

- Don't wear makeup for a day.
- Have dinner delivered.
- Plan a surprise date with someone you love. Plan exactly what you would want planned for you. Enjoy the gift of time out!
- Have coffee or tea somewhere new.
- Call a friend who always builds you up and makes you laugh.
- Go see a movie alone.
- Let go of that mistake. It's over!
- Plan a half-hour to gripe about your day. Set the timer and when it goes off, you must shut up and move on with your night.
- Give yourself a gift. You know what you want; let yourself have it.
- Start a gratitude journal and write five things in it each day.
- Put self-affirmations on your mirror.
- Take a walk.

- Say you are sorry right away when you know you are wrong, and then you will have no time to beat yourself up.
- Ask for forgiveness and then accept that forgiveness and move on.
- Pray.
- Set five goals. Be excited about where you are going.
- Be your own cheerleader
- And be gentle!

There are thousands of other ways to be gentle to yourself. We all do life differently and what works for one of you will not work for another. Yet we all can find ways to be gentler with ourselves. We are hard on ourselves mentally, physically and spiritually. We need to back off and be okay with life just as it is. We need to quit the mental rat race and let the gentle thoughts flood our conscious thought lives. Our thought life controls everything we do, and it makes up who we are. It can be changed, and it can be a positive force in our lives. Don't let your own self destroy your own self. There is enough in life trying to destroy you. Don't contribute to your own death.

Our physical beings need a gentle touch as well. We don't get enough sleep, we eat junk, we drink too much caffeine, and we run constantly. Our bodies can't take the self-abuse we put them through. They need a break. We have been given only one body. The better care we take of it, the better it will be to us. We need all the energy and health we can get to accomplish the things we want in life.

Girlfriend, we have a lot of life to live. Let's not sabotage our future. Let's not contribute to our own failure. We are our own judges and jury, we convict ourselves endlessly, and we sentence ourselves to lives full of self-criticism and failure. We need to stop being a judge and start being our own cheerleader! We can't change others and what they think of us, but we can change ourselves. We can change how we treat ourselves. The gentler we are to ourselves, the gentler we will be to those around us. They deserve our gentleness and so do we.

Exercise—Ya Gotta!

I have spent most of my life being overweight and hating exercise. I was the fattest girl in grade school, the slowest runner, the most uncoordinated and, by the time I got to junior high, I had the biggest boobs you'd ever seen. I obviously was not popular or sought out by the boys.

I was teased about my weight constantly. I was miserable and spent a great deal of time alone. I also spent lots of time defending myself. "I don't care if I'm fat! I'm just big-boned! I have a large frame! I just like to eat." And on I would go. But then I would feel awful because I knew the things other kids said about me were true. I knew I was fat and I hated it. I hated putting on a swimsuit. I looked terrible in all my clothes. I was hungry all the time. I hated going to gym class.

I was constantly frustrated and I would make up any possible excuse for not exercising.

To add insult to injury, I got pregnant at 16 and gained 100 pounds. I was huge! It was uncomfortable to be that young and that huge. But I didn't care—or at least I pretended I didn't. I had never exercised in all my life and I truly believed exercise was for other people—not for me. I knew I couldn't even run one block.

At 17 years of age I topped the scales at 225 pounds. By 19, I became desperate. I joined a health club but must confess that, at first, I just went and walked around. I'd watch other people work out and then maybe I'd go into the hot tub. I had this huge mental block with exercising. I just couldn't do it.

After playing "workout" for a while, I just quit going all together. But the bill for the club kept coming every month, of course. "I'm too busy," I told myself. "I get enough exercise the way it is. I'll do it later."

Finally, later came! I began to obsess about my size. I felt icky all the time, none of my clothes fit, and I was depressed. I had to do something! I had shopped at the large-size shop one too many times and I couldn't take it anymore. So back to the health club I went and, this time, I actually began to do some workouts. I had a trainer set me up and measure my body. That measuring part just about put me over the edge. The woman taking the measurements was a size 3 and she had no clue what being overweight was all about.

But I put aside my embarrassment and went to work. I forced myself to go to the gym three to five times a week and each time I went I did a little more and tried a little harder and I actually began losing a few inches.

Over the next three years I lost 70 pounds. I never went on a diet or took any pills. I just kept going to the club and eating sensibly. Oh, I still had to have chocolate but I didn't gorge like I used to. I was feeling better and I didn't eat constantly like I had before. I wasn't hungry all the time and I didn't want the junk I used to. I was treating my body well and it knew what it wanted—water, veggies, fruit and smaller portions.

I was amazed! I was losing weight and feeling good. WOW!

As I lost weight, I realized that I was not "big-boned" and that I felt much better being thin. I felt like a new person.

Not only did the exercise help me lose weight, it helped me feel better about myself. It helped me to eat better. It helped me relieve stress and it gave me a new outlet for **me**.

We all complain and hate exercise. Yet we have to do it for our own good. It doesn't matter what your body size or shape, we can all benefit from regular exercise. Exercise will not hurt you and it **will** improve your life.

I know there are many of you who already exercise regularly. Give yourself a pat on the back and keep up the good work. Those of you who do not exercise—you need to! I know it's not easy. It's hard—you may have to dig way down inside and pull out every ounce of discipline you have. You may never learn to love it but it will make your life better. You will be healthier, happier and more balanced.

Start small, Girlfriend. You will not run a marathon tomorrow. You can exercise in moderation and you can find time for it. We all lead busy lives. We all have stress and craziness. Yet there are a few minutes in a day to take a walk or a few hours in a week to work out. You have to make it a priority. I write "EXERCISE" in my planner three times a week and then I know I will do it. (I'm kind of anal with my schedule. If it's written down, I have to do it!)

Find what works for you. How can you make it happen? What can you do to motivate yourself? I think the keys are to find an exercise you like and to start small. Try walking twice a week for a month. Set aside time and do it. Start with realistic expectations and then stay committed. If you start too big it won't happen.

Be creative. There are many ways to exercise. You can ride your bike to the video store. You can go golfing for an afternoon. You can take a swim. You can jump rope. You can turn on the stereo and dance your little heart out. You can mow the lawn with the push mower. You can shovel the snow from your driveway by hand. You can go skating on a newly frozen lake. You can do whatever you like to do—just do it. The more physical activities you find that you like, the more you will look forward to doing them. At least, if you choose things you like it won't be total torture!

If it has been a long time since you exercised, I encourage you to visit your doctor first. It's a good idea to get your doctor's input prior to starting a new physical activity.

I have to confess that I still go through phases where I hate exercising and it takes everything in me to stop what I am doing and do it. Yet I do it because I have to and I know I need to. I am truly blessed when I get to the club because I see all of my girlfriends there. They need me there just as much as I need them. We spur each other on to healthier, happier lives.

I have not given myself the option of not exercising. I have to do it for me and I will continue to do it to encourage you.

Make Friends With Your Body—No Matter What Size It Is

Size is a huge thing for many of us, if not all of us! I believe if you polled 100 women, 90 would admit they don't like their bodies. As a society we spend a great deal of time thinking about being fat, about cellulite or about how our bodies look. We are experts at critiquing our own bodies—and the bodies of others, as well. Stupid, isn't it? We waste so much time on our outer woman and we invest so little time on the inner one.

If I were to tell you that I have mastered the body image thing, I would be lying. I wish I could tell you that I was free and that I had a magical way out for you. Yet I have nothing to offer but the truth.

The truth is I am still obsessed. I exercise like a crazy woman, eat sporadically, and I drown in guilt. I feel guilty when I eat too much or when I do not exercise. I freak out when my clothes don't fit and I cry when I try on swimsuits. I hate it! I hate the fact that no matter how hard I try I cannot become friends with my body.

I have read every book on the market, tried every exercise on the planet, and I have affirmed myself to death. I have made repeated vows I would not cut myself down and I have failed.

I actually feel I may be worse than I was before because not only do I struggle daily with my body image, now I know I shouldn't be doing it—and that adds more guilt. All this guilt is crazy and self-defeating, and I have tried everything under the sun to get rid of it. I have tried to pray it away, wish it away, think it away, exercise it away, affirm it away and yell it away. Yet it does not leave.

The area of weight is an extremely sensitive issue because we all compare and secretly torture ourselves. We want to be thinner, be in better shape, want our stretch marks to go away—whatever.

I go through times when it is worse, when I compare myself to every "body" that walks by, to every magazine model and every thing I can. Yet I always come up short and I always want what these other women have.

I cannot measure up no matter how thin I am. I want to be free. I want to be friends with my body. I want to look at myself for who I am on the inside and not for what pants size I wear.

I have been every size from a 6 to a 22, and I experienced a wide spectrum of feelings and received many mixed messages from others as I moved from size to size. It showed me how deeply ingrained the issue of weight is within our culture.

I had always been overweight and had never been very attractive. I was not popular in high school, I didn't fit in, and I never had dates or boyfriends. I felt very alone and was often teased about my weight. I hated what I looked like. I felt there was no hope.

As I grew into adulthood, I made a decision that I was going to make peace with myself if it killed me. I had to let go of the expectations, the negative self-talk and accept me for me. As I did this, I began to like myself for who I was and I began to lose weight. I exercised and I felt good—better than ever before. I tried new things. I had a few dates, and the world seemed more accepting of me. I was more accepting of myself.

My goal started as just a commitment to accept myself as I was. As I accepted who I was, I lost weight. I took care of myself and took risks—all because I began to like me.

But then this new feeling went too far. I became full of pride. I kept losing weight and became obsessed with my new body. I felt that now I had arrived; I was finally there! Being thin was awesome for a while and I enjoyed every minute of it. But then the old tapes started to play again.

This time they were different but the feeling was the same. I found new role models to look at and began to feel inadequate once again about how my body looked. I thought that being skinny would make life wonderful and that, once thin, I would no longer struggle with my body or how I looked. I was wrong!

I felt trapped into caring about a body that I professed to be comfortable with. I wanted the world to think that I didn't struggle anymore. I know many of you do the same thing. We pretend to be okay with ourselves and yet we continue comparing our bodies to those we see on TV. We somehow try to measure up. Yet what are you trying to live up to? What do you want to be? Do you want to be a size 5? Do you think it will make you happy? I know that losing weight makes a difference in how you feel, but it won't remove the quirks. We're all still bothered with our bodies.

I know that I am human, that I am not perfect, that I have along way to go, and that I am way too intense. Do I always change? No—but I do make small steps. I no longer treat my body badly. Even though at times I hate the way it looks, I no longer abuse it. I no longer give the obsessive thinking all my strength. I have some strength of my own now and I am able to pull out of it sometimes and actually laugh at the craziness of it all.

Not one of us is without issues. We all have them. If your issue is losing weight or getting in shape or just being comfortable with your body, then I encourage you to begin dealing with it. Yet before you begin, you need to set some goals. Be realistic, honest and find your own comfort level.

The way I determined my comfort level was to ask myself these questions: How much food do I want to give up? How much time do I want to devote to exercise? What are my pleasures in life? Do I like to eat out? Do I really want to change? Where am I going to be in 10 years? How do I feel when I get dressed or when I am in a bathing suit? How do I feel most days? What is my energy level? What am I willing to do if I want to change my body size? How much will it cost?

Try writing these things down and really looking at them. You may decide to leave your size alone and that's okay because once you have made that decision you do not need to obsess anymore. You weighed the pros and cons and you came up with the answer, "I like the way I am."

If you decide that you really want to make changes, then go for it! Set realistic goals but start where you are right now, not where you want to be in two months. Start small and reward yourself often. Throw away the scale so you do not fall into the temptation of *that* daily ritual. Be more concerned with how you feel than with a certain number on the dial. Round up your girlfriends to support you and go for it! You can do it and I am excited for you, no matter what you decide to do with your size. Size is irrelevant if you feel good about yourself.

We need to stop being consumed with others and let ourselves go. I am on the journey to finding freedom from this issue and I invite you to come with me. We can grow together!

Michelle Neujahr, Speaker

Whether it is a keynote or a full-day seminar, Michelle Neujahr is the challenge your audience needs. She works with people who want more, people ready to live the life they have imagined.

When Michelle speaks, audiences are transformed and ready to move out of their comfort zones and into their lives.

Michelle is the passionate spark your team needs.

For booking information call 800-958-6513
Or visit us online at *www.Michelle Neujahr.com*

Encourage others to join you in living passionately real. Ask your local bookseller for copies of *Hey, Girlfriend!* or visit www.amazon.com. To order in volume, call Milt Adams at Beaver's Pond Press at 952-741-8818.

We'd love to hear from you! Send your comments, stories and victories to us so we can celebrate with you.

Hey, Girlfriend!
P.O. Box 833
Forest Lake, MN 55025

HeyGirlfriend@michelleneujahr.com

All the Best,
Michelle Neujahr

Order Form

To purchase additional copies of *Hey, Girlfriend!* for yourself or to send as a gift, please fill out the form below:

Number of books (U.S.)	_____	x	$14.95 _____
Number of books (Canada)	_____	x	$19.95 _____
Shipping per book	_____	x	$3.00 _____
Sales Tax (MN residents only)	_____	x	$0.97 _____
			Total _____

Ship to:
Name:_____
Address:_____
City: _____ State: _____ Zip: _____
Phone: _____

Call for quantity discounts. Sorry, no credit cards.
Make checks payable to Michelle Neujahr. Please remit in U.S. funds.

Call, mail or fax your order to:

Hey, Girlfriend!
P.O. Box 833, Forest Lake, MN 55025
toll free 800-958-6513 • fax 651-982-4917 • business phone 651-982-2893

If you would like Michelle Neujahr to write a personalized message in your book(s), feel free to fill in the name of the addressee(s) and any other words below:

_____
_____
_____